*"I went thither to lay
the foundation of a
free colony for all mankind"*
William Penn

PENNSYLVANIA

. . . . .a commemorative portrait

A BICENTENNIAL COLLECTION OF THE HARRISBURG PATRIOT-NEWS COMPANY

PENNSYLVANIA
. . . . .a commemorative portrait

by NICK T. RUGGIERI

text by JOHN M. BAER

Published by
the PATRIOT-NEWS COMPANY
harrisburg, pennsylvania

Manufactured in Pennsylvania, U.S.A.

First Printing, 1975

Library of Congress Catalog Card Number 75-21055

Edited by Marion W. Milliron

Illustration Cutlines by Thomas Coolidge

Color Separations and Printing by R.J. Bojalad Printing Co., Inc., Beaver Springs, Pa.

Type set in Palatino by Batsch Company, Inc., Camp Hill, Pa.

Bound by Maple Press Co., York, Pa.

Acknowledgements

While it would be virtually impossible to give credit individually to all the people who assisted me, I am anxious for them all to know their help in furnishing photographs, booklets and slides aided materially in the preparation of my paintings.

There are several, however, to whom I am especially grateful. I owe a tremendous debt to my publisher, John H. Baum, who made it all possible. I would also like to especially thank Tom Coolidge for his necessary suggestions and for helping me put this book together. In addition, I'd like to express my gratefulness to Al Freistak for accompanying me hundreds of miles as I searched for subjects to paint.

Also, I would like to thank William Lunsford and his entire staff, and Ray Dotter of the Community Service Department; the staffs of the William Penn Memorial Museum and Archives, the Pennsylvania Department of Commerce, the Bureau of Travel Development and the Pennsylvania State Library; and my able assistant, Rodney McClure.

To
Rose and Rosemary

Foreword

Pennsylvania As I See It—

States, like people, have distinct personalities that are the result of long years of hard labor and human ingenuity. People from many lands with different backgrounds have shaped the individuality of Pennsylvania.

There is drama in the historical wealth and the beauty of Pennsylvania. I have tried to capture the spirit of this unique state in scenes that evoke the memories of its past and the promise of its future, scenes that reflect the beauty of the countryside and the heritage of religious freedom which William Penn established.

Down through the years, the people have created from forest and vast mineral and water resources a way of life that today depends more on industry than on the soil for its varied livelihood.

It is hard to capture a real portrait of Pennsylvania. This state is a land of great variety in terms of its history, its geography, its landscapes, its people and its cultures. In presenting this portrait of Pennsylvania, I have barely touched a few subjects of its historical past.

Industrial commissions will often deaden an artist's creative expression. The Bicentennial Pennsylvania project left the choice of subject matter and the technical execution entirely to the artist. I cannot imagine any more generous challenge.

Rich as is its heritage, I have tried in the main to paint Pennsylvania as it is today and hopefully will continue to be tomorrow.

All in all, it is a portrait of a great state.

Nick T. Ruggieri

September 1975

Dear Readers:

   It is with great pride that the Patriot-News Co. presents *Pennsylvania: A Commemorative Portrait.* As the nation nears its 200th birthday it is fitting that the newspaper of Pennsylvania's capital city contribute to the celebration.

   Our state has played a vital role in the founding and growth of our country. It is the seat of American history. And it should be commemorated fully as we prepare to pay homage to our national heritage in 1976.

   Words alone are not enough to tell the story of Pennsylvania. What it was and is we therefore present through the eyes of the artist. We feel that the genius of Nick Ruggieri has captured once and forever the beauty and history of the Commonwealth. He has brought a history book to life, and has paid a great tribute to his home state.

   The diversity of Pennsylvania, while adding greatly to its stature, historically has contributed to regionalism prevailing in politics, lifestyles and art. For the first time, we offer a comprehensive work of art for all of Pennsylvania. We offer a living memorial to all of the state's counties.

   It is our hope that this union of art and history will help all who see it discover or rediscover the real Pennsylvania. On the eve of America's Bicentennial, we present a true portrait of our great state.

Sincerely,
JOHN H. BAUM
Publisher

COMMONWEALTH OF PENNSYLVANIA
OFFICE OF THE GOVERNOR
HARRISBURG

GREETINGS:

All of us who love our Commonwealth of Pennsylvania will be most appreciative of the magnificent portrayal of its greatness as exemplified in the 76 Bicentennial Art works executed by Nick Ruggieri including, as the collection does, at least one depiction of each of our state's 67 counties.

These splendid works of art, portray the almost indescribable beauty of our Commonwealth's scenery, the gradeur of its cities, the stirring development of its industries and the moving representation of its historical past. These paintings are a tribute to the dedicated efforts of one man, Nick Ruggieri, of whom we are justifiably proud.

Truly, these are representative paintings — historical, scenic, contemporary — even provocative. These are a portrait of Pennsylvania, and they should bring greater appreciation of our Commonwealth and provide new inspiration for countless thousands — young and old — who view these works of art.

The collection represents public service of exceptional merit. I commend Mr. Ruggieri for his patient and devoted efforts and the Patriot-News Company who is sponsoring the exhibitions throughout the Commonwealth, for making these works available to be viewed by our citizens and our visitors during the Bicentennial Year.

MILTON J. SHAPP
Governor

"Art brings life to life," said John Sloan, one of Pennsylvania's most famous artists, and that is how Nick Ruggieri is celebrating his native state and the 1976 Bicentennial with these 104 paintings of his Commonwealth. This book is the culmination of Ruggieri's 50-year career in art.

Beyond his craftsmanship, diligence and care, an artist must have a sense of awe for what he sees, experiences and imagines. Pennsylvania is a big and varied state, with a multitude of different people and a kaleidoscope of wonders. It is to Ruggieri, as it was to William Penn, a special part of "God's great fat earth."

Ruggieri spent almost three years in researching and preparing sketches for this book. In actuality, he has put into it the five decades of art from his life's experience and the 35 years he has been the art director of the Harrisburg Patriot-News. This book is literally a window on Pennsylvania, created from the love of Nick Ruggieri for art.

A founder of the Harrisburg Art Association in 1927, a long-time teacher of art, a Fellow of the Royal Society of Art, and an indefatigable contributor to the culture of his community and Commonwealth, Ruggieri has been as unselfish of his talent as he has been a master of it. Like so many fine artists, his work gets richer as the years go by.

This book is, in effect, a guest tour of Pennsylvania conducted by Ruggieri.

He once described himself as an "impressionistic realist." And he commented, "Painting is always an experiment. A painting can have all the abstract forces at work within it, all the precious qualities of pigment and surface, all the personal calligraphic lines of strength — and at the same time tell a story or make a statement."

Nick Ruggieri would call this cavalcade of Pennsylvania in 1976, this song in color, an "experiment" of artistic skills. It is that, of course, but it is one that has succeeded far beyond even his own expectations and high standards. Future Pennsylvanians will find it a rare and enduring accomplishment, as a whole and for specific paintings, and it will be experienced by them with all the joy that it is by us.

PAUL B. BEERS,
Author:

Profiles from the Susquehanna Valley
Published by Stackpole Books.

14

The Commonwealth of

5th day of 1st 1681

". . .this day my country was confirmed to me under the great seal of England, with large powers and privileges, by the name of Pennsilvania, a name the king would give it in honour of my father. . .'Tis a clear and just thing, and my God that has given it to me through many difficultys, will, I believe, bless and make it the seed of a nation. . ."

William Penn

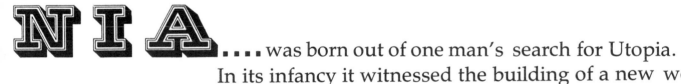....was born out of one man's search for Utopia.

In its infancy it witnessed the building of a new world.

It was reared in the Revolution. It survived the strife of civil war. And it grew to be an industrial giant, a keystone among states. Within its borders lies an open history book that shows how it was "the seed of a nation."

It was founded by William Penn, a converted Quaker, a philosopher and a seeker of better worlds, who wanted land in America to conduct a *"Holy Experiment."* He wanted to offer an alternative to the religious and political suppression of Europe. He wanted to build a new government, based on tolerance, offering justice with mercy.

17

And it all began because neither Penn's father, Admiral Sir William Penn, nor King Charles II of England took the advice of William Shakespeare about lending and borrowing. In lieu of a 16,000 English pound debt owed to Penn senior, Charles granted to William Penn in 1681 almost all the land that is now the Commonwealth of Pennsylvania.

Penn submitted the name *"Sylvania,"* or *Woods*, but Charles requested the prefix *"Penn."* When it was pointed out to Penn that his family name was derived from the Welsh word "penn," meaning highland, an appropriate tag for the mountainous terrain had been acquired.

With more than 28 million acres in his domain, Penn at the age of 36 was made the largest landholder in the British Empire, with the exception of the crown.

The land given to Penn was once ocean floor. Later it was a land of mountains, of forests and of Indians. Today, it measures 45,126 square miles. Its average length, east to west is 285 miles, and its width, north to south, 156 miles. It is one of four commonwealths in the United States, including Massachusetts, Virginia and Kentucky. It has 67 counties and more cities than any other state.

Nothing is written about Pennsylvania without the mention of its diversity. Rich in natural resources, and richer in history, the state has everything. The only thing it never had was a homogeneous population.

At various times, it has been under the foreign control of the Netherlands, Sweden, the French military and Great Britain. Its people have been, and still are, Indians, Dutch, Swedish, Finnish, English, Welsh, German, Swiss, Scottish, Scotch-Irish, straight Irish, French, Italian, Jewish, Greek, Armenian, Austrian, Hungarian, Polish, Czechoslovakian, with an infusion of African and Oriental.

The first real settlers within Pennsylvania's present borders were Swedish. Johan Printz, named governor of the province by Queen Christina, established the first local governments and the first courts in 1643 on the Delaware River at Tinicum, southwest of what is now Philadelphia.

There he built a fort and carried on a fur trade with the Indians. He ruled New Sweden for 10 years, and before returning to Europe gave his daughter in marriage to his successor, Johan Papegoja, in what is believed to be the first Christian wedding within the state's borders.

Two years after Printz went back to Europe, the Dutch, under Peter Stuyvesant, uprooted the Swedes. In 1644, the English established supremacy, and the province was ruled by the Duke of York until 1682, when he formally turned over Pennsylvania to William Penn.

On August 31, 1682, a man three times imprisoned—once in the Tower of London—for his views concerning religious freedom, a man expelled from Oxford for espousing the Society of Friends, or Quakers, set sail from England to claim his new land. The voyage took nearly two months. He first visited Upland, the temporary capital, and renamed it Chester. He went to the present site of Philadelphia where, in accordance with his instructions, the city streets were being laid out and the first homes were under construction.

Now in the land of the Indians, he met with chiefs of the Lenni Lenape, Susquehannock and Shawnee tribes. He promised coexistence, explaining that his religious beliefs forbade the use of weapons or violence. He extended an offer to live "in peace and friendship." And he extended it beyond the Indians.

In the preface to his *Frame of Government* for the new province, he wrote ". . .any government is free to the people under it where the laws rule, and the people are a party to those laws." He established a bicameral legislature, and at its first session, in December of 1682, saw it adopt an Act of Union for all territories within Pennsylvania's borders and an Act of Naturalization, whereby the Dutch, Swedes and Finns residing in those territories were made legal citizens of his Commonwealth.

Penn's promise of a just government, with tolerance for all—coupled with offers of land at easy terms—brought colonists to Pennsylvania by the thousands. By 1685, the province had 7,000 citizens. The *"Holy Experiment"* was underway, and the state that would grow out of it began to take form.

English Quakers settled in the southeastern counties. Germans began to populate the interior counties. The Scotch-Irish frontiered their way into the Cumberland Valley, then westward. The Irish, Dutch, Swedes, Welsh, French Huguenots and others added to the mixture and helped make colonial Pennsylvania the first real *"melting pot"* in America. The pot simmered through 80 years of colonization. Boundary disputes, a revolution in England, a brief deprivation of Penn's power and the natural growing pains of a colony were added to the broth.

By the eve of America's Revolution, Pennsylvania was the third largest of the original colonies, even though it was next to the last to be founded. Its counties grew in number and extended westward beyond the Allegheny Mountains. Its population exceeded a quarter of a million citizens. Then the pot boiled over. A thirst for independence from England covered the colonies. And the people of Penn's woods would help lead the way to nationhood.

Pennsylvania provided more leaders and played a more dominant role in the shaping of America than any other colony. Its major city,

Philadelphia, became the capital of the Revolution. The first and second Continental Congresses met there in Carpenter's Hall and in the State House respectively. The Declaration of Independence (bearing the names of nine Pennsylvanians: *Benjamin Franklin, James Wilson, John Morton, Robert Morris, Benjamin Rush, George Clymer, James Smith, George Taylor* and *George Ross*) and the Constitution of the United States were signed there. When the Articles of Confederation, adopted in York in 1778, were replaced by the Constitution in 1787, Pennsylvania was second to ratify the new law of the new nation.

Pennsylvania farmers had battled for independence. Pennsylvania resources were essential to the colonial cause. Its farmlands supplied food for troops. Its factories turned out munitions. And its people traded blood for freedom.

Historians believe that the American flag first saw battle in Pennsylvania, at Brandywine. It was at Valley Forge where George Washington and his troops nearly froze before going on to win a crucial victory after crossing the Delaware River. Pennsylvania was essential to the creation of the Continental Navy, many of whose ships were built in Philadelphia and manned by Pennsylvania sailors. A door to the great Northwest was opened by Oliver Hazard Perry when he won a major naval battle near Erie during the second war with England.

Pennsylvania is history. It has been blessed and cursed by those events that make history. Within its borders was fought the bloodiest and most decisive battle ever waged on United States soil. After three days at Gettysburg—July 1, 2 and 3, 1863—the Civil War had been won and lost, and more than 51,000 Americans had been killed, maimed or listed as missing there. Pennsylvania Governor *Andrew G. Curtin* approved plans to establish a national cemetery at the site. At the dedication of that cemetery, President *Abraham Lincoln* delivered a 10-sentence address that went unnoticed. But the simple eloquence of his words will outlive us all.

During the ordeal of World War II, Pennsylvania sent its sons and daughters to serve in both hemispheres of the earth and turned its industrial power to producing the materiel of battle. So great was the impact of the output of its factories that the state was labeled the *"Arsenal of Democracy."*

Today, with its history still being written, Pennsylvania can boast of that same diversity that has contributed so much to America.

It remains rich in the farmlands that fed settlers and revolutionaries. A large portion of the state is rural, and produces dairy and livestock products, as well as grains, fruit, tobacco and other crops. The mineral resources of the Commonwealth have made it a major coal-producer, both anthracite and bituminous. Petroleum, natural gas, clay products and glass also are produced in Pennsylvania.

The Keystone State, so named because of its geographical position among the 13 original colonies, is one of the major manufacturing centers of the world. Its steel and iron production is its largest single industry. But the manufacture of aluminum, textile and chemical products, plus electrical machinery, construction equipment, food products and leather products also are a part of its industrial life. These resources helped to shape a nation, helped to protect its rights and helped to nourish the seed planted by William Penn.

Its history and its resources; its lakes and its factories; its mines and its pastures - all of these and much more combine to present a portrait of Pennsylvania. No single picture could ever tell the whole story.

John M. Baer

The Commonwealth of Pennsylvania 67 Counties. . . . .

Adams

Adams County, located in the south central region of the state, is a combination of natural beauty and national history.

Its county seat, Gettysburg, was the site of the most decisive battle of the Civil War, and the bloodiest ever waged on American soil.

The Battle of Gettysburg is remembered in Adams County with some 16 museums, a national park, more than 2,000 monuments and the battlefield itself—25 square miles of countryside set aside in homage to those who died there more than a century ago.

Gettysburg also was the site of Abraham Lincoln's eloquent address, delivered in 1863 at ceremonies dedicating the Gettysburg National Cemetery.

Much of the beauty of the county is provided by its rolling countryside and its miles of fruit orchards. It is one of the leading apple districts in the United States, and is first in Pennsylvania in apple production. Among the county's most festive holidays are Apple Blossom Sunday—the first Sunday in May—and Apple Harvest Day—the second Sunday in October.

The county itself measures 526 square miles and is named in honor of President John Adams. It is bordered on the west and north by mountains, and on the south by the state of Maryland. In 1763, amid controversy over whether the land belonged to Maryland or Pennsylvania, two British surveyors—Charles Mason and Jeremiah Dixon—established the boundary line that would later separate the states of the North and the Confederacy of the South during the nation's Civil War.

Among the county's famous sites is the farm of the late President Dwight Eisenhower, located just south of Gettysburg.

25 *APPLE BLOSSOMS—Springtime brings to Adams County orchards mile upon mile of the billowing apple blossoms for which the area has become famous.*

Left—GETTYSBURG BATTLEFIELD—The guns now stand silent on this battlefield where the greatest artillery duel and cavalry battle on the North American continent was fought in 1863. Over 51,000 men were killed or maimed in the three-day battle which decided the destiny of America.

APPLE STILL LIFE—A dominant industry in Adams County, apple growing utilizes the area's natural resources to nourish Americans. It has made Adams County the Commonwealth's largest apple-producing county.

27

Allegheny

"The Point" where the Ohio River is formed by the confluence of the Monongahela and Allegheny Rivers is the center of Allegheny County in more ways than one.

Today, that "point" is called *"The Golden Triangle,"* in Pittsburgh, and is one of the best known business and industrial centers in the world. Geographically, it is in the middle of the 730 square miles that make up the county.

Allegheny County, located in the western part of the state, probably was named for the Allegewi Indians. Pittsburgh is the county seat and the greatest iron and steel producer on earth. The blazing furnaces of its *"Steel Valley"* put out most of the steel and pig iron used in America. It also is known as the *"City of Bridges,"* with a dozen spans in its downtown area.

The county, like many in the Commonwealth, is representative of the state. Although it is best known for its iron and steel production, it also is rich in mine and quarry products, particularly bituminous coal, as well as agricultural crops such as corn, wheat, apples and potatoes.

In addition to its fame as a manufacturing center, Allegheny County has had its share of history. George Washington was the first to recognize the value of "the Point," and suggested construction of a fort on its site. Eventually, Fort Duquesne played a prominent role in the French and Indian War. The Ohio River made Pittsburgh the largest inland port, and served to connect it with New Orleans. By 1834, with completion of the Pennsylvania canal system, Pittsburgh became a gateway to the West. The Pittsburgh Gazette, the first newspaper west of the Allegheny mountains, hit the streets on July 29, 1786. And the first Republican convention was held there in 1856.

Today, Pittsburgh ranks third in the nation as headquarters for industry, hosting more than 100 major corporations.

Among the county's points of interest are the Mellon Institute of Industrial Research, the *"Cathedral of Learning"* at the University of Pittsburgh, the Buhl Planetarium, one of the largest in America, and the Carnegie Museum. Some of its most famous citizens have included Dr. John A. Brashear, astronomer and educator; Stephen C. Foster, composer; George Westinghouse, Henry Clay Frick, A.N. and R.B. Mellon, industrialists, and Andrew Carnegie, business tycoon and philanthropist.

STEEL MILL ON THE MONONGAHELA—*Easy access to fields of bituminous coal and ideal location at the headwaters of a vast water transportation system have made Pittsburgh the greatest iron and steel producing center the world has ever known.*

29

BARGES—*Barges are used to transport coal to the mills to produce iron and steel. The coal barges travel Allegheny County's 8,000 miles of navigable waters, including the Allegheny, Monongahela and Ohio Rivers, to deliver their resources.*

31 GOLDEN TRIANGLE—*The confluence of the Monongahela and Allegheny Rivers was a strategic location during the struggle for control of the Ohio Valley in the 18th century. Today the site is one of the world's greatest business and industrial centers, Pittsburgh.*

CATHEDRAL OF LEARNING—*The 41-story, 545-feet-high skyscraper of the University of Pittsburgh, the "Cathedral of Learning" is the only skyscraper university in existence. On the cathedral's left is the Heinz Memorial Chapel.*

BLAST FURNACES—Blast furnaces are used to change natural resources into finished iron and steel. This blast furnace helps Pittsburgh to be the greatest iron and steel producer in the world.

Armstrong

Armstrong County, like much of Pennsylvania, is blessed with an abundance of mineral resources. It is a western county named for Col. John Armstrong, an Indian fighter credited with clearing the way for colonial settlements there.

The county is best known for its production of plate glass. At Ford City, named for the father of the plate glass industry in America, John B. Ford, is a huge glass plant that employs thousands of residents. Bituminous coal is mined in the county in quantity and natural gas is produced in many parts of the county, which measures 660 square miles.

Kittanning is the county seat and the site of what was once one of the largest Indian settlements in the state. The borough's name was derived from the Indian "at the great stream," the Allegheny River.

Early settlers of Armstrong County were primarily Scotch-Irish and Revolutionary War soldiers who were given grants of land in payment for their military service. The county was formed in 1800 from parts of Allegheny, Lycoming and Westmoreland Counties.

Iron and steel sheets, fire clay products - including the famous Kittanning bricks - chinaware and a variety of agricultural products are produced in the county.

It is covered by thousands of acres of forests, plateau lands and farms. It is riddled with mountain trails, many predating colonial settlers, and its river park along the Allegheny at Kittanning is one of the most beautiful waterfronts in the state.

COAL MINERS—Miners dig deep in the earth to extract bituminous coal from the soil of Armstrong county. Coal is one of the minerals which is found in abundance in the county.

Beaver

Bordering on Ohio, Beaver County has shared in the industrial progress common to many of Pennsylvania's western counties. It is a steel and iron producer that also is covered with farmland. Like most of its neighbors, its prosperity has been due to the combination of agriculture and industry.

It was named for the Beaver River, which, like Beaver Creek, Beaver Falls and Beaver, the county seat, honors the animal that heavily populated the area during its early history.

Beaver pelts probably accounted for much of the county's initial commerce, and were used by the Indians for barter with white traders in the region. As Pittsburgh, southeast of Beaver County, began to grow in importance, so did the principal waterways in the county, the Ohio and the Beaver Rivers.

Today, the county has a huge steel mill in Aliquippa, one of the world's largest structural steel plants in Ambridge and the nation's first commercial atomic power plant in Shippingport.

Beaver County's best known tourist attraction is Old Harmony, a restored compound that was an experiment in communal living during the 19th century.

Located near the present site of Ambridge, it is a memorial to the Harmony Society, a colony of celibate workers whose agricultural and industrial products contributed greatly to the development of western Pennsylvania.

35 OLD ECONOMY VILLAGE—The third and last home of an early experiment in communal living and industry, Old Economy was built by the Harmony Society in 1825 under the leadership of Father George Rapp.

Bedford

As a south central county formed before the Revolutionary War, Bedford is rich in the frontier history of Pennsylvania. Many of its early leaders took part in forming the new nation. And through its borders rolled the famous Conestoga wagons carrying settlers farther west.

It is named for the Duke of Bedford, and although its boundaries were laid out in 1766, it was not made a county until 1771. It once covered almost all of southwestern Pennsylvania. Its present land size is 1,018 square miles and it borders the state of Maryland.

Bedford, the county seat, originally was named Raystown after Robert Ray, the area's first white settler. Fort Bedford, one of the strongest outposts in colonial Pennsylvania, was built there in 1758 and played a major role in the French and Indian War and the Pontiac Wars.

General George Washington had troop command headquarters at the Espy House in Bedford during the 1794 Whiskey Rebellion. The house, located almost in the middle of the borough, still stands.

Just south of Bedford is Bedford Springs, a well-known health resort and once the "Summer White House" of Pennsylvania's only president, James Buchanan.

Bedford County produces mine and quarry products, lumber and bituminous coal. Its agricultural products include rye, wheat, oats, livestock, poultry—especially white turkeys—and wool.

LANDSCAPE WITH COWS—*An abundance of water from springs and brooks has made Bedford County an ideal location for cattle grazing on the numerous fertile farms which dot the county's landscape.*

Berks

Formed from parts of Philadelphia, Lancaster and Chester Counties in 1752, Berks was named by the Penns for Berkshire, England. It is the birthplace of Daniel Boone and the home of Abraham Lincoln's ancestors.

The county is as rich in history as it is in fertile farmlands. It was first settled by the Swedes, who were joined around 1700 by Quakers, German Amish, French Huguenots and Mennonites. Raging battles between Indians and white settlers marked its early history. Today there are memorials to Conrad Weiser, an Indian interpreter and peacemaker, and to Shikellamy, counsellor of the Six Nations Indians, both of whom worked for an end to the frontier wars.

The first iron forge in Pennsylvania was established in Berks County in 1716, and Thomas Mifflin, the Commonwealth's first governor—serving from 1790 to 1799—fought as a general from Berks County during the Revolutionary War.

Reading, home of the Reading Railroad, is the county seat. Berks covers 864 square miles and is well known for its fruit orchards and rolling farmlands.

Berks County is a leader in the manufacture of textiles and textile machinery, with large plants located at Wyomissing. There also is a brick plant there, one of the largest in the East. And metal production is a major industry.

Among the historical highlights of the county are the colonial home of Conrad Weiser, near Wormelsdorf; Daniel Boone House, near Baumstown; Friends Meeting House, built in 1730; Pine Forge, the first iron mill in the state, built in 1725; the site of Fort Henry; and the homestead where Abraham Lincoln's ancestors were born.

DANIEL BOONE HOMESTEAD—Daniel Boone was borne in this log cabin in Berks County, November 2, 1734. His father, a weaver and a Quaker, settled here as early as 1730. Like his famous frontiersman son Daniel, he was a pioneer in a primative settlement.

Blair

Although the area that is now Blair County was settled long before the Revolutionary War, its real expansion was directly attributable to completion of the Pennsylvania Railroad in 1852, connecting Philadelphia and Pittsburgh.

The Scotch-Irish first settled in the region, establishing a number of communities along the eastern slopes of the Allegheny Mountains. But it was the construction of railroad lines over those mountains that brought rapid expansion and prosperity to the area.

The world-famous Horseshoe Curve, west of Altoona, is an engineering marvel. The curve is 2,375 feet long, and around its 91 feet per mile grade the mainline trains moved westward, bringing industry and progress in Blair County.

The largest railroad shops in the world were built in Altoona, and repair and construction of railroad cars and locomotives provided employment for thousands of county residents.

Blair County was named for John Blair, a prominent advocate of public improvement projects and the only native-born Pennsylvanian to have a county named after him.

The county seat is Hollidaysburg, named in honor of the pioneer Holliday Family, which was massacred by Indians.

In addition to its railroad industry, the county also produces paper and textiles, coal and dairy products, as well as a variety of agricultural crops. It covers 530 square miles, and the mountains throughout provide its scenic beauty.

HORSE SHOE CURVE—A world-famous engineering achievement, the Horse Shoe Curve of the Penn Central Railroad in Blair County is 2,375 feet long and has a grade of 91 feet per mile. It opened in 1854 when westward expansion demanded a mainline connecting east to west.

Bradford

If Marie Antoinette had escaped France and the guillotine, she had a home waiting in Bradford County. French noblemen in 1793 established a community they named Asylum. *"La Grande Maison,"* and buildings surrounding it, were to provide a new life in the New World for the queen and other French refugees of nobility. Some of them made it to America, and their descendants and mementoes are still found in the region.

Bradford County, bordering on New York State, originally was named Ontario. It was established in 1810 and named for William Bradford, who was U.S. Attorney General under President George Washington and who also served as the attorney general of Pennsylvania.

The area was populated heavily by the Iroquois and Munsee Indians, and their history there is both valuable and ancient.

Towanda, located along the North Branch of the Susquehanna River, is the county seat. Bradford's rough mountains and fertile limestone valleys give it a diversified terrain. The Wyalusing Rocks, overlooking the Susquehanna valley, provide a classic Pennsylvania landscape.

The county measures 1,147 square miles. It is a leader in the production of buckwheat, hay, honey and milk. Large quantities of milk are transported from Bradford to metropolitan areas, especially New York City. The county is covered with forests and famed for miles of dogwood blossoms in the spring

WYALUSING ROCKS—The Wyalusing Rocks gracefully overlook the North Branch of the Susquehanna River Valley in Bradford County. Iroquois Indians, who named them the "prayer rocks", came to the Wyalusing Rocks to receive inspiration from nature's beauty.

Bucks

The home of William Penn and the starting point of George Washington's famous crossing of the Delaware River, Bucks County is one of the most historic parts of an historic state.

Located in the southeastern part of the state, it is one of the three original counties in the Commonwealth, and Penn himself named it for Buckinghamshire, England. Local government in Bucks County dates back to 1680. And in the county court house at Doylestown are land deeds issued by Penn beginning April 1, 1681.

Pennsbury Manor, home of the famed Quaker, is reconstructed and an historic drawing card. A monument now stands at Washington's Crossing to commemorate Christmas Eve, 1776, and a rout of the British at Trenton.

The county, measuring 617 square miles, is separated from the state of New Jersey by the Delaware River.

It was first settled by English Quakers, many of whom had crossed the Atlantic with Penn aboard the *Welcome*. It is the home of the Delaware Canal and the site of many early Indian treaties.

Textile plants are located throughout the county, and Bristol is a major center for chemical and aircraft parts production.

One of the first schools ever to teach scientific farming was opened there in the 1830's, and agriculture, especially the growing, canning and marketing of vegetables, is a major industry.

The county also is a cultural center for writers and artists, and its *Art Colony* at New Hope is known throughout the East.

THOMPSON-NEELY HOUSE—Built in 1702, the Thompson-Neely House served as headquarters for General Lord Stirling, Captain William Washington, Captain James Moore and Lieutenant James Monroe. They held conferences here for planning of the Delaware Crossing on Christmas night, 1776.

DELAWARE CANAL AT NEW HOPE—Completed in 1832, the Delaware Canal was designed to transport coal cheaply from the Lehigh Valley to Philadelphia and New York. The canal was closed in December, 1931, but the portion of the canal at New Hope in Bucks County has been preserved.

Butler

Once the heart of the Commonwealth's frontier region, Butler County, northwest of Pittsburgh, was settled primarily by Pennsylvanians moving westward from other counties.

The area was purchased from the Indians in 1784 and was organized as a county in 1800. Many early residents were Revolutionary War veterans who accepted land grants in payment for their service.

Harmony, in the southwest section of the county, was the original site of the Harmony Society and was one of three communal colonies founded by the Rev. George Rapp.

John A. Roebling, a native of Prussia, founded Saxonburg in Butler County, and in the 1830's invented wire rope there. His invention was used for the Portage Railroad on the Pennsylvania Canal and also led to the building of suspension-type structures. Roebling became one of the foremost engineers in America, and designed the *Brooklyn Bridge.*

Butler, the county seat, led the nation in the manufacture of small, lightweight motor vehicles, and has the distinction of inventing the "jeep."

The county covers 794 square miles and is rich in natural gas and petroleum. There are oil refineries and huge manufacturing plants in Butler County. Iron and steel production is a major industry and dairy farming is a growing one.

The county and its seat are named for General Richard Butler. There are 33 townships in Butler County and all but six of them each measure five miles square.

OLD STONE HOUSE—*Few counties were organized under more pioneer conditions than Butler County, organized in 1800. Many early settlers stopped at local water holes to prepare their horses for the trip into the new region.*

Cambria

Charles Dickens, in his *"American Notes,"* talks about Cambria County and his ride on the Portage Railroad in 1842. The railroad ran from Hollidaysburg, in Blair County, to Johnstown, the largest city in Cambria County, connecting the eastern and western sections of the Pennsylvania Canal.

A majority of Cambria County's early settlers were Welsh, and when the county was formed in 1804, it was given the ancient name for Wales - Cambria.

Demetrius Augustine Gallitzin, a Russian prince, rejected his title to become a Roman Catholic priest in 1795 and dedicate his life to settlers and Indians in the Cambria County region. He built a log cabin for a chapel at Loretto in 1800, and today parks and monuments bear his name.

The county, measuring 695 square miles, is, like most western counties, a mining and steel center. The first commercially-produced steel rails in the country came from Cambria County, and the first tilt-top steel converter was used there in 1861. The county seat is Ebensburg.

In May, 1889, the notorious Johnstown Flood claimed 3,000 lives and destroyed $25 million worth of property. The city, surrounded by mountains, was decimated when the South Fork Dam, a reservoir of the Pennsylvania Canal, broke 16 miles above Johnstown.

Among the county's points of interest are the Incline Plane, which is 896 feet long, at Johnstown; a monument at Cresson marking the birthplace of Admiral Robert E. Peary, discoverer of the *North Pole;* and the first railroad tunnel built in the United States.

INCLINE PLANE—Johnstown today is the site of the famous Incline Plane or Sky Ride, which is nearly 900 feet in length. Built as a lifesaver after the flood of May, 1889, it later achieved its purpose and carried 4,000 persons to safety during the flood of March, 1936.

Cameron

When President Abraham Lincoln called for strong northern men to fight for national union in the Civil War, lumberjacks from Cameron County put buck deer tails on their hats, met at Driftwood and rafted down the Susquehanna's West Branch to enlist in Harrisburg. Expert hunters and marksmen, they became known as the *Bucktail Regiment* and were renowned for their strength and courage. A monument pays them tribute at Driftwood.

Cameron County is one of the north central counties, sparsely populated and covered with forests and game preserves.

It was formed in 1860 and named in honor of U.S. Senator Simon Cameron, a Pennsylvania statesman who served for a time in President Lincoln's Cabinet. The county seat and only town of any size is Emporium. It is the home town of Gen. Joseph McNarney, who commanded U.S. forces in the Mediterranean during World War II. And it is the home of one of the largest radio tube and electronic equipment plants in the east.

Flagstone is a natural resource peculiar to Cameron County. It is of such high quality that it was chosen for Arlington National Cemetery and for the walkways leading to the Tomb of the Unknown Soldier.

In its early days, the county relied almost exclusively on lumber for its commerce. More recently, other industry and the development of agricultural and dairy products have added to its prosperity.

Cameron County is among the hunting, fishing and scenic areas most visited in Pennsylvania.

LUMBERING—*One of the finest wooded areas in the Commonwealth, Cameron County has over 200,000 acres of forest land. The heavily-timbered region became an attraction for lumbermen after the Civil War. Today, trucks still transport the area's lumber to American manufacturers.*

Carbon

Historians say anthracite coal was discovered under some tree roots in Carbon County by Philip Ginter in 1791. The county is named for its principal product, and large anthracite deposits within its borders led to development of the state's coal industry.

Mauch Chunk, Indian for *"Bear Mountain,"* is the site of the county seat and the site of one of the first railroads in America. It was made of wooden rails and connected the coal mines on Summit Hill with the Lehigh River and waiting barges. It was powered by gravity with mules to haul the cars back up the nine-mile stretch to the mines. Mauch Chunk was renamed Jim Thorpe when the famous athlete was buried there.

The Carbon County area was settled first by Moravian missionaries. The county was formed in 1843 and covers about 400 square miles.

The Lehigh River cuts the county in half, twisting through its mountains to form the Ox Bow Curve, one of many natural wonders in the Commonwealth.

A mining and farming area, Carbon County is known for its rugged, majestic mountains. Jim Thorpe sits among those mountains and has been called *"The Switzerland of America."*

One of the "coal region" counties, Carbon also is regarded as an excellent dairy farming area.

RAILROAD STATIONS—One of the first railroads in America was built to connect the Summit Hill coal mines with the Lehigh River by way of Mauch Chunk. Today the town is Jim Thorpe, and historic railroad stations such as this one remind the county's people of their past.

45

Centre

Located in the geographical middle of the Commonwealth, Centre County is the home of The Pennsylvania State University. The school stands amid the Nittany Mountains, named for the Indian princess, Nita-a-Nee.

Bellefonte, the county seat, is regarded as *"The Home of Pennsylvania Governors"* (Curtin, Beaver, Hastings and Bigler). Its name comes from the French for *"Beautiful Spring,"* and just south of it is *"Fishermen's Paradise,"* an area on the Spring Creek renowned for its large and numerous trout.

The county, measuring 1,115 square miles, was formed in 1880, and immediately became prosperous through its iron industry. The Centre Furnace, near State College, was erected in 1791, and Andrew Carnegie built the foundation of his own iron industry at Scotia.

Boalsburg, in the southern part of the county, is said to be the birthplace of Memorial Day, and a shrine there pays tribute to the 28th (Keystone) Division of both world wars.

Centre County is rich in Indian history, and was the home of Bald Eagle, a prominent chieftain, whose name a mountain and creek bear, and Logan, the son of Shikellamy, whose name also appears on geographical features.

The county has been known widely for its bituminous coal, mined in its western section, as well as for limestone, metal products, matches and ceramics. The manufacture of brass and bronze also is a major industry.

Penn's Creek begins in an all-water, limestone cavern that is one of the principal tourist attractions of the area.

OLD MAIN—The oldest building on the main campus of the Pennsylvania State University, Old Main was built in 1859. The institution is the Land Grant College of Pennsylvania, created by the Commonwealth under the Land Grant College Act of Congress in 1862.

Chester

Valley Forge, the site of the Battle of Brandywine, and the largest mushroom houses in the country are in Chester County. It's an area packed with history and industry. Located in the southeastern section of the state, it is one of the three original counties.

William Penn laid out Chester County in 1682 after buying the land from the Indians. It is named for Cheshire, England. Parts of the county border on the states of Maryland and Delaware, and it measures 760 square miles.

The Revolutionary War's Battle of Brandywine was fought at Chadds Ford, and Valley Forge Park, marking the site where George Washington's army spent a frozen winter of 1777-78, is partly in Chester County.

West Chester, originally named Turks Head, is the county seat. Kennett Square, in the southeastern part of Chester County, is renowned for its extensive mushroom growing and the beautiful Longwood Gardens.

Iron and steel production vies with agriculture for the top industry of the county. Large steel mills at Phoenixville and Coatesville produced armaments for two world wars. And the fertile soil throughout the county produces all types of farm products to feed nearby urban areas.

Historic sites in Chester County include Chester Springs, where a Continental Army hospital was established during the Revolutionary War, and Laurel Forge, where the iron sides of the famed Civil War gunboat the *Monitor* were made.

Next Page HOPEWELL VILLAGE —*Active from 1770 to 1883, Hopewell Furnace in Chester County provides its visitors a picture of the humble but ingenious beginnings of the iron and steel industry. It also provides a striking contrast for measuring the growth and magnitude of this basic industrial enterprise.*

ST. PETER'S VILLAGE — Established as a quarrytown for the mining of black granite during the Civil War, St. Peter's Village has been preserved as a picturesque community.

49

GROWING MUSHROOMS—A mushroom farmer checks the beds of mushrooms in his farm with the aid of a helmet lamp. Chester County is the national center of the cultivated mushroom industry, producing over 65 million pounds annually.

OCTAGONAL SCHOOLHOUSE—Known as the Diamond Rock School, this unusual octagonal schoolhouse near Paoli was built in 1818, and was restored 100 years later. It is believed the school was built in this form for heating benefits from a centrally-located stove.

Clarion

It was not until after 1800 that about 150 pioneering Scotch-Irish hacked their way through the western wilderness to establish the first settlements within the present borders of Clarion County.

They lived primarily by farming, and later built a number of small saw mills that produced lumber they riverboated down to Pittsburgh. Pine tar from the knots of pine trees also was shipped to Pittsburgh, and the revenue raised was used to buy the tools and other goods needed to develop a wilderness.

Clarion County was formed in 1839. It measures about 600 square miles, and, like its county seat - Clarion - is named for the Clarion River, which bisects the county.

Mineral deposits there led to the development of an iron industry that flourished during the Civil War and later gave way to the steel industry. The manufacture of glass - there is a large bottle factory at Knox - and the mining of bituminous coal contributed substantially to the area's growth.

The Clarion River, which winds its way through the county's vast forests, provides miles of scenic area. The county is a well-known hunting and fishing region and it retains much of its unspoiled land, including a stand of virgin timber in Cook Forest State Park in the northeast corner of the county.

VIRGIN PINES—With over 159,000 acres of forest land, the virgin pines and hemlocks of Clarion County long have attracted lumbermen to the area. Cook Forest, situated mostly in Clarion County, has the largest stand of virgin white pines east of the Mississippi River.

51

52   CREEK WITH BOAT—*The unspoiled land of Clarion County provides a scenic background for this boat as it rests on the shore of one of the county's many lakes.*

Clearfield

The Rev. John Ettwein, an eighteenth century Moravian missionary who worked among the Indians, described in his personal journal on June 14, 1772, a place "where the buffaloes formerly cleared large tracts of undergrowth so as to give them the appearance of cleared fields. . ."

It is not known whether the Rev. Ettwein or the Indians gave Clearfield County its name, but it's plain that the once-numerous Pennsylvania buffalo were responsible for it.

Like many of the state's "younger" counties, Clearfield was once a wilderness populated by large Indian tribes. Its present county seat, Clearfield, formerly was the important Indian town of Chinklacamoose.

The county is located in the upper part of the Susquehanna Valley's West Branch, and timbering was for years its most profitable industry. As rich in natural resources as it is in Indian history, the county soon developed into an area that produced coal, clay, iron ore and a variety of farm goods.

It was formed in 1804, and settled by Quakers, French and Germans. It is known for its leather tanning plants, its forests and its hunting and fishing areas. Sabula Lake, the Susquehanna River and two state forest parks attract many campers and visitors.

CANOEING ON LAKE—Glendale Lake in Clearfield County, one of Pennsylvania's largest lakes, is a spot for enthusiasts of all types of water sports. It has an unobstructed run of almost eight miles for canoeists and has a shoreline of more than 26 miles.

Clinton

The Pennsylvania canal system, which was an initial and significant boost to the state's growth, was particularly important in Clinton County.

The area is named for Governor De Witt Clinton, of New York, who himself was a main advocate of canal construction. Lock Haven, the county seat, is so named because of a lock provided there by the canal and a haven provided by the West Branch of the Susquehanna River for timber rafts. Because the town was located at the terminus of the canal and on the Susquehanna, it was an important inland port for timber and other goods being shipped downstream to Williamsport and Harrisburg.

Clinton County was formed from parts of Lycoming and Centre Counties in 1839. Before the Revolutionary War, "Great Island," in the middle of the West Branch of the Susquehanna River, was the site of a large Indian town. The island's especially fertile soil yielded some of the finest tobacco crops in the state.

Maple syrup has long been a Clinton County product, with much of it coming from Sugar Valley, an area in the southern part of the county, named for groves of maple trees.

The county has forests, rich farm lands and mineral resources. It covers 902 square miles.

On July 4, 1776, the men of Pine Creek in Clinton County gathered under the "Tiadaghton Elm" and declared their personal independence from England. At about the same hour that day, other men were adopting another declaration in Philadelphia.

HYNER VIEW—Hyner View, a beautiful panorama of the countryside near Renovo on the West Branch of the Susquehanna River, is a landmark of the Bucktail State Park. The park was named after the famous Civil War Regiment of woodsmen, the Bucktail Rangers.

Columbia

COVERED BRIDGE—Part of the county's 25 covered bridges, this one remains in Columbia providing Pennsylvanians a glimpse of the picturesque bridges of years past.

Columbia County was named to honor a patriotic song, "Hail Columbia," written by Joseph Hopkinson during the War of 1812.

The county has been a state leader in the manufacture of metal products and textiles. The first all-steel railway cars made in America came from plants at Berwick. And at Bloomsburg, the county seat and the only incorporated "town" in Pennsylvania, is located one of the largest carpet factories in the nation.

Columbia County has history too. It was once the camping grounds of the Delaware and Shawnee Indians. In 1864, more than a thousand federal troops were sent to the Fishing Creek Valley to break up an alleged conspiracy by draft dodgers who were supposedly building a fort of their own to resist induction into the Civil War. Some men were arrested in "the Fishing Creek Confederacy," but later released for lack of evidence.

One of the famed Molly Maguire murder trials was held in Bloomsburg in 1877. The Molly Maguires were coal miners who, as a secret organization, gained great power in the 1860's and 1870's, fighting for improved conditions in the mines and using every method available to do so.

The county is laced with waterways and is bisected by the North Branch of the Susquehanna River. Columbia only covers 484 square miles but is an area well-known for its scenic beauty. Among tourist attractions are Profile Rock, Rickett's Glen and the 1780 Quaker Meeting House near Slabtown.

TWIN BRIDGES—Covered Bridges once provided settlers with the means of crossing Columbia County's waterways. Today, the Twin Bridges still stand over one of the many branches of the Susquehanna River which flows through the region.

Crawford

In an area known for its natural beauty and commercial productivity, Crawford County covers 1,016 square miles. It is located in the state's northwest, and borders along the Ohio state line.

It is named for Colonel William Crawford, a friend of George Washington, who was burned at the stake by Indians in 1792. The county was formed in 1800.

Metals, textiles, chemicals, oil, dairy goods and potatoes are among Crawford's major products. The county prospered greatly when oil was found in the area by Colonel Edwin Drake in 1859. Titusville, just about a mile from Drake's first well in Venango County, became an oil boom town and all of Crawford County had an important role in developing an industry that would revolutionize industry itself.

Conneaut Lake, just west of Meadville, the county seat, is the largest natural lake in Pennsylvania. It's three miles long and two miles wide, and is a popular summer resort.

The state's largest water recreation area and wild fowl sanctuary is at the reservoir of Pymatuning Dam along the county's western border. The lake is 16 miles long and covers about 16,000 acres.

John Brown, the famed abolitionist, ran a tannery near New Richmond from 1826 to 1835. And President William McKinley was a student at Allegheny College in Meadville. The school, established in 1815, is the oldest college in northwest Pennsylvania.

DRIFTWOOD ALONG THE LAKE —Meaning "Crooked-mouth man's dwelling place," Pymatuning Lake is the second largest man-made lake east of the Mississippi River. As sailboat enthusiasts enjoy its waters, its shores provide an ideal setting for a study in driftwood.

Cumberland

The sixth county to be established in the Commonwealth, Cumberland County occupies an area of south central Pennsylvania that witnessed pre-Revolutionary War growth and the ever-westward movement of the state's pioneers.

The county was formed in 1750 and was populated originally by Scotch-Irish settlers who were first to move into the Cumberland Valley. It is named for an English shire, and Carlisle has been the county seat since 1752.

Despite its inland location, Cumberland County has much military history. It was once frontier land, dotted with forts, and instrumental in the French and Indian War. Carlisle Barracks is among the oldest military posts in the nation, and the area hosted Generals John Armstrong and George Washington and produced armaments for both.

Revolutionary War heroine Molly Pitcher of the Battle of Monmouth, N.J., is buried in Carlisle. During the Civil War, the city was occupied by Confederate Troops and was considered to be of great strategic value. The Carlisle War College today is an important military school for military brass, and nearby, at Mechanicsburg is one of the largest Naval supply depots in America. Carlisle also was the site of the famous Indian School.

Carlisle was the home of three signers of the Declaration of Independence, George Ross, Thomas Smith and James Wilson, who became a U.S. Supreme Court Justice. Dickinson College, in Carlisle, was founded in 1783 as only the twelfth college chartered in the United States. Carlisle also has had the prestigious Dickinson Law School since 1834.

Colonial homes and monuments are seen throughout Cumberland County. Most of its 555 square miles is rural. Among its many points of interest are First Presbyterian Church, built in 1757; the old county courthouse; and a relic iron furnace at Pine Grove.

HESSIAN GUARDHOUSE-ARMY WAR COLLEGE—Built as a powder magazine in 1777, this building was first used to store all powder from Baltimore when that Maryland city was threatened during the Revolutionary War. It was most likely converted to a guardhouse in the early 1800's and is now a museum at the Army War College in Carlisle.

59

LAUGHLIN MILL—One of the most colorful and oldest mills in the region, Laughlin Mill near Newville dates back to 1763. An old grist mill, it is typical of late 18th century buildings.

Dauphin County, the site of the state's capitol, is an area of geographic and historic importance dating back to the 1720's.

An early trade route along the Susquehanna River brought, among others, John Harris, a native of Yorkshire, England, to the area. He established a trading post and ferry across the river. And Harris' Ferry or "John Harris' Place," is designated on the earliest British maps of central Pennsylvania.

When Harris died in 1748, his son, also John, took over the trading business, became an expert Indian negotiator and a leader in the Revolution. He donated the land for and personally laid out

the city of Harrisburg, the county seat, in 1785. It has been the state capital since 1812.

Dauphin County has been a major transportation and commercial center throughout its history. The Rockville Bridge, north of Harrisburg, is the longest stone arch railroad bridge in the world, measuring 3,830 feet across the Susquehanna River. The Pennsylvania canal began in Harrisburg when on July 4, 1826, ground was first broken there for the canal system.

Steel mills in Harrisburg and Steelton nearby; coal mines in the Lykens Valley and the world-famous Hershey Chocolate Corporation contributed to the county's prosperity.

Dauphin, named for an heir to the French throne, also had military significance as marked by the Indiantown Gap Military Reservation and a former massive air base at Middletown.

Middletown is the oldest town in the county and was so named because of its position halfway between the older sites of Lancaster and Carlisle.

The county measures 520 square miles and includes such historic sites as the John Harris Mansion, built in 1776 and once occupied by Simon Cameron; the Old Paxton Church, built in 1740; the gravesite of the first John Harris; and the state capitol and museum.

Dauphin

61 PAXTON CHURCH—William Bertram was installed as the first pastor of this church in 1732 at Paxtang. He was succeeded by the famed "Fighting Parson" John Elder. John Harris Jr. is buried here along with other leaders of the area.

MILLERSBURG FERRY—*The colorful stern-wheelers, the Roaring Bull and the Falcon, cross the Susquehanna River daily between Liverpool and Millersburg, reminding Pennsylvanians of an era past.*

Next Page—ROCKVILLE BRIDGE— —Nearly 13 football fields in length, the Rockville Bridge is the largest stone arch railroad bridge in the world. The Penn Central span crosses the Susquehanna River, connecting Dauphin and Perry Counties.

MILLERSBURG SQUARE—*The gazebo was a center of activity for Millersburg residents as they gathered in the square for community activities. It still stands in the Millersburg square today.*

63

Left—CAPITOL DOME—*The Pennsylvania State Capitol dome, which towers 272 feet and weighs 12 million pounds, is surmounted by a figure holding a garlanded mace— —symbolic of the Commonwealth and its government. It was dedicated in October, 1906.*

Delaware

Delaware County was the site of the first permanent settlement in Pennsylvania. Swedish pioneers, under Colonel Johan Printz, moved there in 1643, forty years ahead of William Penn's Quakers.

The area, named for the Delaware River, which borders its southeast, was the first in the Commonwealth visited by Penn. His provincial government was established at Upland, the first capital, which he renamed Chester.

Delaware County is a populous area loaded with industry. There are giant oil refineries at Marcus Hook and huge shipyards at Chester. Farming, especially truck farming, also is important, and like its western neighbor, Chester County, Delaware County produces large mushroom crops.

Chadds Ford, in Delaware County, was the scene of the Battle of Brandywine during the Revolutionary War. At Radnor is the burial place of General "Mad" Anthony Wayne, a Revolution hero, and at Swarthmore is the birthplace of artist Benjamin West.

The county is one of the smallest in Pennsylvania, measuring only 185 square miles. Parts of it border on Philadelphia and the state of Delaware. The county seat for many years was Chester, but it was moved to Media, which is located in its center.

Among important historical spots in Delaware County are the Caleb Pusey House, the oldest in the state, built in 1683; the restored birthplace of Declaration of Independence signer John Morton; and a memorial marking the site where William Penn began his "Holy Experiment."

COLONIAL COURTHOUSE —Built in 1724, the Delaware County Courthouse is the oldest public building in continuous use in the United States. The Declaration of Independence was read publicly for the second time here in 1776.

Elk

Vast mountains and endless forests cover this northwestern county, and have lent to it the means for prosperity through wood and mineral products.

Elk County, established in 1843, is named for the large herds of elk that roamed the region during its early history. The area still is a haven for wildlife and is among the most popular hunting and fishing land in the Commonwealth.

Leather goods and paper products supported the county for decades. Wilcox Tannery once was the largest in the world. It is estimated that more than a million buffalo hides were tanned there between 1866 and 1876 alone.

Ridgway is the county seat and a center for production of electrical machinery and leather items. Saint Mary's and Johnsonburg are the other main cities, and are known for carbon products and paper products, respectively.

A German Catholic Brotherhood organization bought some 35,000 acres of the area in 1842 and much of the county remains predominately Catholic. At Saint Mary's the first Benedictine convent in America was established.

In addition to its miles of forests, Elk County has bituminous coal, natural gas and oil. It is an area that retains a large section of its virgin timberland.

SWINGING BRIDGE —Elk County residents used to rely on swinging bridges such as this one to cross difficult terrain. The region is covered by vast mountains and forests.

Erie

The northwestern-most county in the Commonwealth, Erie borders on the Great Lake for which it is named and, in part, on the states of New York and Ohio.

Lake Erie's importance as a link to the Allegheny, Ohio and Mississippi Rivers, as well as to the northwest, made the region valuable as a military stronghold and a commercial center.

Commodore Oliver Hazard Perry led his fleet against the British in the Battle of Lake Erie on September 10, 1813. His victory gained Americans sole access to the great Northwest and is among the most heralded naval fights in our history. After it, he issued his famed message: *"We have met the enemy; and they are ours."*

Founded in 1800, Erie County covers an area that witnessed numerous Indian wars. Both the county and the lake are named for the Erie Indian Tribe.

Erie, the county seat and largest city, is the home of the Erie Canal. The city has a large harbor and is the state's only lake port. It also is the home of one of the largest electrical plants in the country.

The French were first to settle the region, and, like France, Erie County's soil yields an abundance of superior grapes. Many of New York state's finest wines are made with Erie County grapes. Cherries also thrive in the county's soil.

Among historical attractions in the county are the Perry Monument, Old Customs House and the restored flagship *Niagara*.

67 *FLAGSHIP NIAGARA—Erie County built the fleet of Commodore Oliver Hazard Perry which on September 10, 1813, defeated the British fleet in the Battle of Lake Erie. His second flagship, the Niagara, twice raised from the bottom of the lake, now stands as a memorial of the battle.*

68 ICE FISHING—Ice fishing has evolved as an extremely popular winter sport in northwestern Pennsylvania. Here, on the frozen surface of Presque Isle Bay at Erie, Ice fishermen enjoy their sport.

Fayette

Fayette County is named for the Revolutionary War hero, General Marquis de Lafayette. It is an area that served as home and haven for many men instrumental in shaping the history of the state and the nation.

General Lafayette and his son, George Washington de Lafayette, visited the county after it was established in 1783. They were hosted at Uniontown, the county seat, by Albert Gallatin, a U.S. Senator from Pennsylvania and a Secretary of the U.S. Treasury.

Philander Chase Knox, a U.S. Senator and Secretary of State, and General George C. Marshall, World War II Army Chief of Staff, are natives of Fayette.

Located in the state's sourthwest, the county made history even before it was established. Fort Necessity was built there by General George Washington in 1754, during the French and Indian War. The Whiskey Rebellion took place in Fayette County, and was quashed when federal troops were sent to Uniontown.

The county produces large quantities of bituminous coal, coke and natural gas. Quarry products also contribute to its commercial value.

Parts of Fayette County border on the states of West Virginia and Maryland. Among the county's points of historical interest are Friendship Hill, the home of Albert Gallatin; the site of Fort Necessity; and the gravesite of British General Edward Braddock, killed in a battle with French and Indians.

69 FALLINGWATER —This home was designed and built by internationally-famous architect Frank Lloyd Wright in 1936. The design employs bold cantivevered construction perched on giant boulders over a rushing waterfall. Fallingwater is located near Mill Run.

Forest

Perhaps the greatest wooded area in the Commonwealth, Forest County is among the most scenic regions in the East.

It is named, of course, for the miles of forest that cover it. Substantial stands of virgin timber flourish within its borders, mostly in the Allegheny National Forest, which covers most of the county, and Cook Forest State Park, part of which is in Forest.

The county is both small and young. It measures only 420 square miles and was not formed until 1867.

The area was settled primarily by Moravian missionaries seeking to convert the Delaware Indians native to the region. As in other northwestern counties, timbering fast became Forest's main industry. And the county's principal waterways - the Allegheny and Clarion Rivers and the Tionesta Creek - lent transportation to rafts floating south with lumber.

Tionesta, the seat of local government, is named for the creek and is the only borough in the county.

There is a large state fish hatchery along the Allegheny River in the western part of the county that produces great numbers of fish to stock the state's waterways.

TREES—Founded in 1848, Forest County has over 200,000 acres of timberland. Much of the wooded land is today part of the Allegheny National Forest.

Franklin

Franklin County is the birthplace of James Buchanan, the only President of the United States from Pennsylvania.

Bordering on the state of Maryland, Franklin County is located in the south central part of the Commonwealth. It covers 754 square miles of Blue Ridge Mountains and peach and apple orchards.

The county is named in honor of Benjamin Franklin. Its first settlers were Scotch-Irish. The area witnessed much of the French and Indian War and parts of the Civil War. Following the Battle of Gettysburg, retreating Confederate survivors passed through Waynesboro on their way south. A year later, in 1864, Confederate cavalry burned Chambersburg.

Chambersburg is the county seat and is named for Benjamin Chambers, a Scotch-Irish pioneer who settled the area in 1730.

Franklin County is a state leader in the growing of peaches and is second only to Adams County in apples. Dairy farming is also an important industry and combines with a variety of manufactured products to give the county its balanced prosperity.

Among its historical sites are the birthplace of President Buchanan near Mercersburg, Civil War sites, the Caledonia Furnace, built by Thaddeus Stevens, and three state parks.

71 PRESIDENT BUCHANAN'S BIRTHPLACE —
Pennsylvania's only gift to the Presidency was born in Franklin County April 23, 1791. The birthplace of President James Buchanan still stands four miles west of Mercersburg.

Fulton

The western neighbor of Franklin County, Fulton was a part of Bedford until formed in 1850. It also borders on the state of Maryland and was the site of the last Confederate camp in the North during the Civil War.

Originally, the county was to be called Liberty, but instead was named to honor Lancaster County's Robert Fulton, the inventor of the steamboat.

Forbes Road and the Pittsburgh and Chambersburg turnpikes—the main routes used by pioneers moving west—passed through Fulton County. Long lines of Conestoga wagons laced the county's hills during its early history. Like much of this area of the state, the county truly was a pioneering region and witnessed many Indian wars.

Fulton County measures only 435 square miles, but its location along the eastern slope of the Allegheny Mountains gives it scenic hills and valleys unsurpassed in the Commonwealth.

McConnellsburg, named for an early settler, Daniel McConnell, is the county seat and the county's only borough. The principal products of the county are buckwheat, livestock and flour. It is an area that is largely rural and a favorite of sportsmen.

CIRCULAR BARN—Nationally known for its buckwheat, the fertile soil of Fulton County has long been the source of its leading industry—agriculture. This circular barn is a unique landmark of those who till the soil to produce the famous crop.

Greene

The Greene County area was among the first in the United States to be settled west of the Allegheny Mountains. Located in the southwest corner of the state; it was the center of boundary disputes for years between the commonwealths of Pennsylvania and Virginia.

Although settlement began in the 1760's, the county was not formed until 1796. It is named for General Nathanael Greene, and its county seat, Waynesburg, is named for Pennsylvania's Revolutionary War hero, General "*Mad*" Anthony Wayne.

Greene County is the state leader in sheep farming, and also has some of the richest bituminous coal deposits in the Commonwealth. Natural gas and oil production also are more established there than in most areas of the state.

The county covers 577 square miles and benefits from the Monongahela River and its tributaries. It is the birthplace of former Governor Edward Martin, who also served as Auditor General, State Treasurer, Adjutant General and an officer in five wars.

SHEEP—The well-watered valleys of Greene County provide ideal conditions for grazing sheep. The county, in the southwestern corner of the state, is by far the Commonwealth's leading sheep producer.

Huntingdon

Selina Hastings, the English Countess of Huntingdon, was a benefactress of the College of Philadelphia which became the University of Pennsylvania. A provost at the school, Dr. William Smith, owned land in the central part of the state, and when he laid out a borough, he named it Huntingdon in her honor.

The county grew from the borough and was created in 1787. The area was once a large Indian settlement called Standing Stone, a name derived from an actual stone erected by the Indians and bearing their art and markings. A replica of the stone stands on Main Street in Huntingdon, the county seat.

Huntingdon County has been a producer of charcoal iron, clay and stone products and some coal. Sandstone hills of up to 100 feet high at Mapleton provide quarries for glassmaking. The Juniata River and the Pennsylvania Canal served to ship these and other goods westward to the large markets of Pittsburgh.

Two Pennsylvania governors, David Rittenhouse Porter and Martin G. Brumbaugh, came from Huntingdon County, as did former U.S. Senator John Scott.

The county covers 895 square miles of rugged Allegheny Mountain ranges.

EAST BROAD TOP RAILROAD — A "registered national historic landmark," the steam locomotive powered train was built in 1873. Today, it is the last narrow gauge railroad operating in the Eastern United States.

Indiana

Around 1812, salt was discovered within the borders of Indiana County, and it fast became a major product. Salt wells were drilled along the Conemaugh River at Saltsburg and the industry flourished until the 1830's.

Indiana County, a western county named for the Indians who lived there, shares a wealth of mineral resources with its neighbors. Like many other counties in this region, it boomed as a coal county even before the Civil War.

The county measures 861 square miles and first was settled by the Scotch-Irish from the Cumberland Valley to the east. A true wilderness in its early days, much of the land merely was survived upon rather than developed. This was true for many years after its incorporation as a county in 1803.

The county seat, Indiana, is the site of lands once owned by George Clymer, a Philadelphia landholder and a signer of the Declaration of Independence.

In addition to salt and coal, Indiana County has produced limestone, natural gas, clay and glass products and rubber tires.

A monument at Cherry Tree, on the eastern edge of the county, marks a 1768 Indian treaty boundary that extended to a cherry tree that stood on the West Branch of the Susquehanna River.

EWING'S MILL—Built in 1838, Ewing's Mill, in Indiana County's eastern hills, is a real working water-powered gristmill. It is believed the McCormick Water Turbine which powers the mill is the oldest in existence.

Jefferson

Punxutawney, the oldest town in Jefferson County, is one of the best known in the state. Every Ground Hog Day, Punxutawney is nationally recognized as the home of the animal who looks for his shadow to predict the length of the winter.

The name Punxutawney is from the Indian for "gnat town." The legend attached to the name says a wizard who lived in a cave was burned alive by the Indians, but that his ashes turned into gnats, or "punkies", to continue guarding his domain by bothering anyone who ventured near.

Jefferson County is named to honor President Thomas Jefferson. It's a northwest county that built its commerce on an early timbering industry. But mining, quarrying, dairy farming and other agricultural business has taken over from the lumber industry.

The county measures 652 square miles, and Brookville is the county seat. The first settlers arrived in the then-wilderness area about 1797, but the county wasn't formed officially until 1804. Even then it was attached judicially to neighboring counties and it wasn't until the 1830's that Jefferson's development began in earnest.

STONE QUARRY—Mining is Jefferson
County's leading industry. Among the resources produced are coal, natural gas and
building stone.

79

Juniata

Named for the Juniata River, this oddly shaped, narrow county benefits from the valley of that river and has some of the richest farming land in the Commonwealth.

All types of agricultural products, and especially fruits, are found in Juniata County. Its location along the old Pennsylvania Canal and later along the Pennsylvania Railroad mainline provided easy transport access and incentives for commerce of all kinds.

The county was created in 1831 from portions of Mifflin County. It was a hunting ground for the Delaware Indians, and the Scotch-Irish settlers who pioneered there as early as the 1740's were constantly at war with the tribe.

Mifflintown, on land originally owned by John Harris and later named for General Thomas Mifflin, is the county seat.

Saw mills and grist mills along the Juniata and its tributaries spotted the county during its development. Today, there is dairy farming as well as quarrying to add to the area's prosperity.

HUNTER—An ideal hunting region used by the Delaware Indians, Juniata County today remains a popular area for hunters who search its countryside for game.

BEERS' MILL—"Merchant John"
Patterson built Beers Mill in 1811. Destroyed
in the flood of 1972, the famous mill has been
owned by the Beers family since the early
1900's.

81

Lackawanna

Located in the very heart of Pennsylvania's coal regions, Lackawanna County is the site of the first underground anthracite mine in the world.

The mine was opened at Carbondale, in the northeast corner of the county, in 1831. The site is marked today by a tablet along a town street. But while mining made the area and always has been a principle industry, Lackawanna County also produces textiles, especially nylon and rayon, plastics and a wide variety of other goods.

Scranton, the county seat, is named to honor the Scranton brothers, George W. and Sheldon T., and their cousin, Joseph H. Scranton, whose financial and business sense contributed greatly to the commercial development of the region.

The city, third largest in the state, has been called Slocum Hollow, Harrison and Scrantonia at various times. Before settlement, it was the site of Capoose Village, home of the Muncee Indians.

The county is covered with natural lakes and has many parks along and near them. At Archbald is the world's largest glacial pothole. And Nay Aug Park is among the most scenic in the commonwealth.

OPEN PIT MINE—Huge anthracite collieries handle the mining and refining of Lackawanna County's coal deposits. The first underground anthracite mine in the world was opened in Carbondale in 1831.

WATERFALL—NAY AUG PARK—The waterfall and grounds of Nay Aug Park are a constant inspiration to those who view its natural beauty.

83

Lancaster

Lancaster County, where farming is an art form, justly is called *"The Garden Spot of the State."* It is the heart of the Pennsylvania Dutch country, and is recognized as having the richest soil in the nation.

Named for Lancashire, England, and created in 1729, the county leads the country in the production of cigar leaf tobacco, and leads the state in corn, barley, hay, wheat, cattle and other agricultural goods.

Pennsylvania's Amish, unique throughout the world, are the county's premier citizens. Passionately dedicated to excellence, their customs, lifestyle and agricultural prowess have remained unchanged, generation after generation.

But the county also has industry - past and present. It is the home of the Conestoga Wagon, which carried those who won the West. And, prior to 1745, the Pennsylvania Rifle, later misnamed the Kentucky Rifle, was made in a small gun shop near the center of Lancaster County. Today, the county produces watches, linoleum cork products, food processing equipment, textiles, lumber, leather and metal goods.

The county covers 945 square miles of the Commonwealth's southeast, and Lancaster, which served as the nation's capital for a few hectic days in 1777 and as state capital from 1799 to 1812, is the county seat.

Among its many points of interest are the birthplace of steamboat inventor Robert Fulton, near Unicorn; Wheatland, the home of James Buchanan, Pennsylvania's only president; and Ephrata Cloisters, buildings erected in the 1730's by a German religious society devoted to labor, meditation and worship; and the vast farmlands of Lancaster County.

BARN—*The amish have for eight or nine generations farmed the richest general farming area in the United States. Lancaster is the Number One non-irrigated county in the United States in the value of farm products sold, traded or used by farm households.*

CLOISTERS —In 1732, Conrad Beissel founded a religious colony known as the Ephrata Cloisters. Beissel insisted on a celibate life for all members of the colony and established Saturday as the day to observe the Lord's Day.

PLANTING TOBACCO—*Named for Lancashire, England, Lancaster County today is known throughout the United States for its tobacco. The fertile fields of the county produce 90 per cent of America's cigar filler tobacco.*

NIGHT SCENE—At night, the farms and communities of the county provide a picturesque scene of peacefulness and beauty.

Lawrence

Located along the eastern border of Ohio, Lawrence County is famed for its production of tin, china and pottery. It is an industrial county that also manufactures iron and metal products, and the confluence of the Mahoning and Shenango Rivers to form the Beaver River at its county seat—New Castle—made for easy access and fast early development.

The county, which measures 367 square miles, is named for U.S. Navy Captain James Lawrence, who is credited with the historic quote, "Don't give up the ship." He died after speaking his way into history aboard the ill-fated *Chesapeake* during the War of 1812.

New Castle was an important Indian settlement, was a vital outpost during the French and Indian War and served as a key station along the Underground Railroad that helped free slaves before the Civil War.

Points of interest in the county include "The Narrows," along Slippery Rock Creek, McConnell's Mill, and Moravia, where Moravian missionaries built the first church west of the Alleghenies in 1771.

McCONNELL'S MILL—Built in 1868 by Thomas McConnell, this grist mill has been completely restored and now stands as a landmark in the state Park named for it, the McConnell's Mill State Park.

Lebanon

Formerly a part of Lancaster County and now a neighbor, Lebanon shares the limestone-rich soil that has made the area the farming capital of the Commonwealth. It's one of the smaller Pennsylvania counties—363 square miles—but it also is one of the most productive.

Lebanon County's main agricultural goods are milk, cereal grains, poultry, peaches, apples and tobacco. A leader in farming, it also has major quarries at Palmyra and Annville, and a 200-year old iron mine at Cornwall that was an important munitions producer during the Revolution. The county manufactures a variety of other goods, but is best known for food products like pretzels and Lebanon bologna.

Lebanon County, like Lancaster, was settled and shaped by Germans who became the famous "Pennsylvania Dutch." Their influence in making Pennsylvania an important agricultural state is immeasurable.

The oldest chartered waterworks in the country was operated as early as 1700 at Schaefferstown, and parts of the wooden pipes used are preserved in the state museum. The oldest canal tunnel in America was built near Lebanon in the early 1800's, and it is estimated that more than 700 feet of solid rock was dug by hand to do so.

The county also has a large military reservation at Fort Indiantown Gap, the Edward G. Martin Reservation, named for a governor and general. It was used for troop training in wartime and is used now for National Guard operations by units throughout the East.

HARVEST SCENE—*Lebanon County farmers till their limestone-rich soil producing agricultural products which make the area the farming capital of the Commonwealth.*

CORNWALL FURNACE—*The magnetic iron of southern Lebanon County was mined continuously for over 200 years, until the 1970's. (The ore here averages more than 50 per cent pure metal.) Cornwall Charcoal Furnace, operated from 1742 until 1883, forged the Lebanon County ore into cannonballs for Washington's army.*

91

Lehigh

Potatoes, peaches and cement brought Lehigh County prosperity, but the Liberty Bell brought it historic fame. In 1777, when British occupation of Philadelphia was imminent, local patriots took the bell from Christ Church tower, transported it to Lehigh County and hid it under the floorboards of Zion Reformed Church in Allentown. The bell was returned to Philadelphia the following year, but Lehigh County had its place in the history books.

Formed in 1812 and located in the eastern part of the Commonwealth, Lehigh measures 347 square miles and is named for the Lehigh River, which crosses it.

It is the state leader in potato growing and a national leader in the production of cement. Fruits, especially peaches, also are exported in large quantity from Lehigh County.

Fries Rebellion, eastern Pennsylvania's answer to the Whiskey Rebellion, took place in Lehigh County. Led by John Fries in 1798, local residents drove away federal assessors who tried to level a "house tax" on window panes. Fries and about 30 others were later convicted of treason, but pardoned by President John Adams.

Allentown, the county seat of Lehigh, is named for Chief Justice William Allen of Pennsylvania. The city is a major producer of silk as well as mining equipment, foodstuffs and iron and steel.

93 *LIBERTY BELL STORY—Following the Battle of Brandywine in 1777, when it was evident the British were going to occupy Philadelphia, patriots under the cover of darkness transported the Liberty Bell from Christ Church, Philadelphia, to the Zion Reformed Church in Allentown. It was hidden under the church floors there until it was safely returned a year later.*

Luzerne

Luzerne County, located in the Wyoming Valley of northeast Pennsylvania, once was the largest county in the Commonwealth. When formed in 1786, it was a little larger than the state of Rhode Island. But it was pared down to its present boundaries in 1878, and now measures 891 square miles.

The county is the throne of *"King Coal."* A good portion of all of the anthracite mined in Pennsylvania comes from Luzerne County. The so-called "stone coal" was used by blacksmiths and in making arms and munitions in the 1700's. But the anthracite industry really began in February of 1808, when Judge Jesse Fell, of Wilkes-Barre, demonstrated that the coal could burn without a draft and thereby would be ideal for domestic heating purposes.

The Wyoming Valley was Indian territory. And the first settlers there were Moravian missionaries seeking converts. Luzerne has been the scene of years of violent boundary disputes, the worst of which almost sent Pennsylvania to war with Connecticut in the 1750's.

The county is named for a French ambassador to the United States, Chevalier de la Luzerne. Wilkes-Barre, its county seat, was the largest city in the Commonwealth to be decimated by the June floods of Hurricane Agnes in 1972.

The Wyoming Monument, in the city of Wyoming, is one of many attractions in the county. It was completed in 1843, and built with every type of stone found in the region. It pays tribute to Wyoming victims of a 1778 Indian massacre.

WATERFALL—RICKETTS GLEN—Over 33 different waterfalls dot the Ricketts Glen State Park in Luzerne County.

COAL VILLAGE OF ECKLEY—In 1913 over 300 coal breakers dotted the 484-square-mile anthracite region of Northeastern Pennsylvania. Today, some breakers remain such as this one in Eckley as a living tribute to the days when coal was king. Coal breakers were used to separate pure coal from impure rocks.

Lycoming

LOGS ON SUSQUEHANNA RIVER—Billions of board feet of Lycoming County logs and lumber flowed annually on the Susquehanna River's West Branch to mills. The logs, ordinarily 150 feet to 300 feet long, were assembled into a raft manned by a crew of two men.

Covering more than 1,200 square miles of North Central Pennsylvania, Lycoming is the largest county in the state.

Like many counties in this region, it was Indian country, and early settlement was erratic and dangerous. The so-called *"Great Runaway"* took place in Lycoming county and involved hundreds of settlers fleeing by raft and boat to Fort Augusta in Sunbury to escape the wrath of an Indian war waged against them.

The French had been the first to brave the area in the 1750's, but settlement didn't really begin until after a major Indian treaty was signed in 1768. Following that treaty, Scotch-Irish and Quakers moved in from the southern part of the state and began to develop a lumber industry that flourished for decades.

Williamsport, the county seat, was called *"Lumber City"* because of the dozens of saw mills that were built in and around it. These mills were fed endlessly by logs rafted downstream on the West Branch of the Susquehanna River and its tributaries.

The county was established in 1795 and was named for the Lycoming Creek, which flows through it. An area of extensive forests and many streams, Lycoming County is a favorite among sportsmen, and especially draws those who like to hunt wild turkey and fish for bass.

In addition to several 1770's forts, attractions in the county include Picture Rocks, which bear Indian art and history, and the Friends Meeting House, near Pennsdale, which was built by the Quakers in 1779.

One of Pennsylvania's Northern Tier counties that borders on the state of New York, McKean is generally accepted to have been the last of the great frontiers in the Commonwealth.

Although it was formed in 1804, it remained a virtual wilderness and served as a hunting ground for the powerful Iroqouis Indians rather than as a land of promise for Pennsylvania pioneers.

Within about 20 years of its birth, however, the county drew settlers from New England and New York and Pennsylvanians from the south-east section of the state. Together they set to hacking a new life out of the wilderness.

McKean was often called "Governor's County" because of the near patriarchal interest that then Governor Thomas McKean took in his namesake. It measures 997 square miles, is very nearly a rectangle and is covered by miles of pine trees. It has the largest single forest acreage of any county in the state, and its western portion is covered by part of the Allegheny National Forest.

The county's commercial development was, of course, dependent for years on the timber industry. But, following the Civil War, Pennsylvania oil and natural gas were found there in great quantities. Both still are produced in McKean County, and both add greatly to its overall prosperity. The Bradford sand stratum, named for the county's largest city, produces the highest grade crude oil in the world.

Smethport is the county seat. And Mount Jewett, at 2,109 feet, has the highest railroad junction in Pennsylvania.

McKean

OIL PUMPS —*Following the Civil War, McKean County experienced an economic boom resulting from the first commercial development of oil in 1876-1878. Today, it is the world's leading producer of Pennsylvania quality lubricating oils.*

Mercer

The iron and steel industry of the Shenango River Valley gave Mercer County its prosperity, but its typical northwestern Pennsylvania terrain has brought it substantial notoriety as a recreation capital and hunting, camping and fishing center.

The mills at Sharon and Farrell produce iron and steel ingots and bars, structural steel and electrical machinery. The huge 300-ton transformers built for the Boulder Dam were made in Mercer County.

Located along the northwest edge of the Commonwealth and bordering on the state of Ohio, Mercer County was established in 1800 and was named in honor of General Hugh Mercer, a Revolutionary War hero slain at the Battle of Princeton in 1777. Mercer had fought, as a captain, throughout the northwest area of the state during the French and Indian Wars.

A large section of Mercer County was designated as "gift lands" for veterans of the Revolutionary War. The early settlers were Scotch, but many Italians came to the area to work on construction of a pipeline from the oil fields of Venango and Butler Counties, across Mercer and on to Youngstown, Ohio.

The county measures 681 square miles, and includes rolling farmlands that are suited for raising sheep and dairy farming. The county seat is Mercer.

Some of the old locks of the Erie Canal Extension can be found in Mercer County, as well as relics of the Underground Railroad, which served Southern slaves seeking freedom in the North prior to the Civil War.

CAMPING—*Mercer County has long been recognized as a hub of recreational development in northwestern Pennsylvania. In addition to camping, for which the county has numerous sites, warm-weather months see Pennsylvanians swimming, boating, water skiing and fishing in Mercer County.*

Mifflin

Mifflin County has served as a crossroads in Pennsylvania since the days when major Indian trails joined within its present borders. The William Penn Highway and the Pennsylvania Canal also passed through the county, bringing it commerce and easy access to larger marketplaces.

The county is centrally located in the state, and although it is small - 431 square miles - it has two vast and fertile valleys that provide both scenic beauty and a variety of agricultural crops. The Juniata and Kishacoquillas Valleys are formed in Mifflin County by the Blue and Shade Mountains along its eastern border, Seven and Stone Mountains along its western border and Jack's Mountain in the middle.

Although the area was settled in 1731, Mifflin County was not created until 1789. It was named for Pennsylvania's first governor, Thomas Mifflin. Lewistown is the county seat, named to honor an early ironmaster, William Lewis.

The Scotch-Irish and the Amish were among the first to settle in the area, a locality plagued by Indian uprisings and other dangers of an exposed frontier.

Among the points of interest in the county are Jack's Creek Bridge, a stone arch built without a keystone; Bird Rock on Jack's Mountain, and the home of Dr. J.T. Rothrock, the "Father of Pennsylvania Forestry," at McVeytown.

Until recent years, one of the largest rayon plants in the world was operated at Lewistown.

JACK'S CREEK BRIDGE—One of the more interesting tributes to early turnpike days is the Jack's Creek Bridge at Lewistown. It is one of a few existing examples of a stone-arch bridge without the usual keystone.

Monroe

A good portion of Monroe County covers an area best known as the Poconos, the most popular resort region in Pennsylvania.

The Pocono Mountains rise to more than 2,000 feet in Monroe County, and serve as the setting for year-round tourism that lures vacationers from throughout the East. The county is covered by the mountains, glacial lakes, forests and gorges of the Poconos and also by the motels, hotels and inns that house its visitors.

Formed in 1836, the county was named for President James Monroe, the fifth President of the United States. It measures 611 square miles and its county seat is Stroudsburg. Jacob Stroud, a hero of both the Revolutionary War and the French and Indian War, was father of the town and originally owned the land where Stroudsburg now stands.

Metal products as well as paper, electrical machinery and textiles are manufactured in Monroe County, and there is some quarrying of sandstone and limestone. But recreation is the byword in the county. Virtually all forms of outdoor recreation are found there throughout the year. Its mountains make it a great ski resort, and its lakes make it a great boating and fishing area.

The famous Delaware Water Gap, where centuries ago the Delaware River wore down the rock of the Blue Ridge Mountains, is in Monroe County and is a natural wonder.

Right — DELAWARE WATER GAP — The Delaware River, which forms Monroe County's eastern boundary, has long given the region natural beauty. One of the most spectacular scenes is the Delaware Water Gap formed in the Ice Age, when the river slashed through the mountains 1600 feet high on its way to the sea.

One of the early southeastern counties in the Commonwealth, Montgomery County is the site of Valley Forge. There, in the winter of 1777-78, some 11,000 starving and freezing patriots under the command of General George Washington beat the weather and later the British to help America insure her independence.

Valley Forge Park, located about eight miles from Norristown, the county seat, is one of the best known and honored shrines in the nation. It covers 2,200 acres and in the spring includes the largest display of dogwood blossoms in the state.

Montgomery County is named for General Richard Montgomery, who captured Quebec and Montreal during the French and Indian War and who was a hero during the Revolutionary War as well. The county is one of 13 in the state named to honor soldiers. Its earliest settlers were Welsh who bought land from William Penn and who were joined later by Germans from the Philadelphia area.

The county was created in 1784 from parts of Philadelphia County, and measures 484 square miles. It is both an agricultural and industrial area that has prospered since colonial times. The Schuylkill River, its proximity to the city of Philadelphia and its rich plateau soil have contributed greatly to Montgomery County's continued growth.

It was the site of the first iron forge in Pennsylvania, built in 1717 by Thomas Rutter near Pottstown. The iron industry has boomed there ever since, and Pottstown still is known for its iron production.

Mill Grove, the estate of artist and naturalist John Audubon is located in Montgomery County, overlooking the Perkiomen Creek, one of the most scenic waterways in Pennsylvania.

There are literally hundreds of historic markers, churches and homes throughout Montgomery County.

Montgomery

GEORGE WASHINGTON MEMORIAL CHAPEL—The Memorial Chapel and Bell Tower, with its carillon of 58 bells, commemorates George Washington and his heroic soldiers at Valley Forge as well as those who in more recent times have offered their lives in service of our country in the great struggle for faith and freedom.

GEORGE WASHINGTON'S HEADQUARTERS—Millions of Americans have visited the hallowed shrines of Valley Forge. Among the sites in the National Park is George Washington's Headquarters, from which he directed his troops as they endured the incredible hardships of their winter encompment of 1777-1778.

Montour

Montour County, although the second smallest in the Commonwealth, has been prominent in trade and industry for more than a century. The earliest roads in its area - the upper Susquehanna Valley - the Pennsylvania Canal and the Pennsylvania Railroad gave it access to markets and greatly enhanced its commercial worth.

The iron industry there was built from rich ore deposits from the Montour Ridge and was centered in Danville. For many years, beginning with the national expansion that took place following the Civil War, the county was a leader in iron production.

Montour County measures only 130 square miles. It was formed, amidst controversy, from Columbia County in 1850, and was named to honor Madame Montour, a famed Indian interpreter.

Danville, the county seat, was laid out by Daniel Montgomery, a Revolutionary War general and pioneer. It is the birthplace of inventor Frank Emerson DeLong, who produced, among other things, the bobby pin, the first folding cardboard box and the electric stenograph.

Perhaps more noteworthy was the invention of Christopher Latham Sholes, of Mooresburg in Montour County,—the typewriter. Sholes worked as a printer's aide at the *Danville Intelligencer,* and after moving to Wisconsin some years later produced the first working model of the typewriter in 1868.

GROVE PRESBYTERIAN CHURCH AND DANVILLE PARK—The Grove Presbyterian Church steeple towers over the Memorial Park and its monument dedicated to those area citizens who died in America's wars.

Northampton

The first Stars and Stripes of the United Colonies was flown at Easton, the county seat of Northampton County, on July 8, 1776. The flag has been preserved and is displayed in the city's public library.

Northampton County was the site of a number of historic events both for Pennsylvania and for the nation. It was created in 1752 and originally covered a good portion of eastern and northcentral Pennsylvania. The county was named for the Earl of Pomfret who lived in Northamptonshire, England, and its current borders surround 374 square miles.

Early settlers were English and Scotch-Irish, but the area also was pioneered by the French, the Holland-Dutch and Germans. Its major cities are Easton and Bethlehem, which it shares in part with Lehigh County and which is famous for its Christmas and Easter celebrations.

Bethlehem was laid out by the Moravians in 1741. It has the oldest pharmacy in America, the tomb of the unknown soldier of the Revolutionary War is nearby, and it had the first fire engine in the country - "The Perseverance," built in London and shipped to Bethlehem in 1792.

Easton's location at the juncture of the Delaware and Lehigh Rivers, along the western border of the state of New Jersey, has contributed to its growth and importance as a trading center. The county is a leader in iron production and is famous for its cement and slate.

Among its places of interest is the Old Sun Inn at Broad and Main Streets, Bethlehem. The inn was licensed by King George of England in 1761, and its register bears the names of George and Martha Washington, Benjamin Franklin and General Lafayette, among others. In Easton, at Fourth and Perry Streets, is the restored 1757 home of George Taylor, a signer of the Declaration of Independence.

SLATE QUARRY—The slate belt, located in northeast Northampton County, has quarried and finished slate that has been used all over the nation and in many far corners of the world.

Northumberland

The first building in the world to be commercially wired and electrically illuminated was in Sunbury, the county seat of Northumberland County. Inventor-genius Thomas Edison installed the lighting system in the City Hotel there and threw the switch on July 4, 1883. The Hotel Edison stands on the site now and displays a bronze plaque commemorating the event.

Northumberland County, formed in 1772, also was the home of chemist Joseph Priestley, who is credited with the "discovery" of oxygen, carbon-monoxide and soda water. The Priestley House, including his library and laboratory, is preserved as an historic shrine in the borough of Northumberland.

The county, vastly important as an outpost area during the French and Indian War, is named for the northernmost shire in England and measures 454 square miles. Sunbury always has been of strategic and commercial value because of its location at the meeting place of the North and West Branches of the Susquehanna River.

Fort Augusta, at Sunbury, was built in 1756 and has been reconstructed in miniature - on a one-to-six scale - exactly as it was.

Northumberland has diversified manufacturing and is part of the Middle Anthracite coal region. Shamokin and Mount Carmel are among the major coal towns in the county.

The area is known for its Indian history and scenic beauty. Chief Shikellamy, ruler of the Six Nations and a renowned negotiator for peace, is buried at Shamokin.

PRIESTLEY HOME—Dr. Joseph Priestley, credited with "discovery" of oxygen, came to America in 1794. His home in Northumberland, where he died in 1804, has been preserved as a historic shrine. In addition to his scientific achievements, Priestley was a leading advocate of freedom in his time.

COAL BREAKER—The Middle Anthracite coal region had its western end in Northumberland County and in 1850 Northumberland became one of the important anthracite-producing counties. Mining remains an important industry today in Northumberland County.

Perry

A south central county measuring 550 square miles, Perry County emerged as an area widely traversed during the state's pioneer days. Settlers moving westward traveled through its borders, and the Susquehanna and Juniata Rivers brought it both commerce and development.

Sherman's Valley, located near the present site of Loysville, was the area of Perry County that developed most rapidly. The construction of Fort Robinson in 1755 as a defense against the Indians is credited with this fact.

New Bloomfield is the county seat of Perry, which was formed in 1820 and named to honor America's first great naval hero, Oliver Hazard Perry, the victor on Lake Erie.

The choice was fitting inasmuch as Perry County relied heavily on its water resources during its early growth period. Not only did the two rivers and their tributaries bring it trade and access, but they also brought water power, which was used to run the many mills throughout the county.

The county is dotted with old mills and iron forges, tucked in among the Tuscarora Mountains on its northern and western borders and the Blue Mountains in its southern region.

Among the county's more prominent natives have been Pennsylvania Governors Beaver and Bigler; John B. Gibson, Chief Justice of Pennsylvania; and Col. Alexander K. McClure, historian, friend to President Lincoln and founder of the Republican Party in Pennsylvania.

SAW MILL—An abundance of water power made Perry County famous early in its history for its lumber mills. Small mills and industries still are located in the area and produce most of its finished lumber.

Philadelphia—the birthplace of a nation, the Athens of Colonial America, the Quaker City, the mother country of Pennsylvania and the *City of Brotherly Love.* More "firsts" for the United States took place in Philadelphia than in any other city in America. As a county, it is the smallest in the state, county and city being the same. But in importance, it is the largest.

It was the "great towne" that founder William Penn ordered to be built. It fast became the most populous area in the state, and the economic, cultural and political core of colonial America.

Philadelphia, named by Penn for a Biblical city in Asia Minor, was the site of the signing of the Declaration of Independence, the first ringing of the Liberty Bell, the convening of the first Congress of the United States, the first sitting of the U.S. Supreme Court, and on and on.

More American history was made in Philadelphia than anywhere else. And Independence Hall, Congress Hall, Carpenter's Hall, and other sites of historic importance are preserved there today.

Philadelphia was the capital of the United States from 1790 to 1800. George Washington's second inauguration took place there. And Betsy Ross was commissioned there to make the first American flag in 1776.

The Quakers, or English Friends, were the first to settle this southeastern part of the Commonwealth, but they were joined soon and en masse by Germans, Scotch-Irish and eventually every nationality in the world.

Philadelphia became a vital port city to Pennsylvania, then grew into a major trade center known throughout the world. It built factories, battleships and textile plants, and quickly was recognized as an industrial and commercial giant in America. Today it ranks fourth in population in the United States.

Its list of "firsts" are unequalled anywhere. It has the first church built in Pennsylvania (Old Swede's Church); the first Hospital in America (Pennsylvania Hospital); the first daily newspaper, the first library, the first zoo, the first permanent theater, the first bank, the first paper mill and the first U.S. Mint. The list is endless. Mint. The list is endless.

In so many things—history, art, music, literature, commerce, manufacturing—Philadelphia has led the state and the nation.

It is a county alive with the things America was, is and will be. It is the history of the Revolution. It is the cradle of American Democracy. It is Philadelphia.

Philadelphia

Right—INDEPENDENCE HALL—In what is America's most meaningful shrine, 56 men affixed their signatures to the Declaration of Independence in Independence Hall, Philadelphia, July 4, 1776. The Articles of Confederation were ratified here in 1778 and the Constitution was penned in the hall in 1787.

OLD SWEDES'S CHURCH—One of the oldest churches still standing in the United States, Philadelphia's Old Swede's Church held its first services in 1700. The congregation of the church was united with the Episcopal Church in 1845.

DELAWARE RIVER BRIDGE —More than 22,000 miles of wire weighing 6,100 tons were used in the construction of the Delaware River Bridge, completed in 1926. One of the longest single-span suspension bridges in the world, it is 1.8 miles long and over 135 feet above water level.

Right—*RITTENHOUSE SQUARE*—One of William Penn's original squares, Rittenhouse Square was once high in the social scale. Today it is still bordered by some of Philadelphia's best known clubs, hotels, churches and apartment buildings.

Pike

Home of Bushkill Falls, the *"Niagara of Pennsylvania,"* Pike County is known for its scenic beauty, glacial lakes and many waterfalls. At 125 feet, Bushkill Falls is among the most impressive in the state. But others in Pike County, like Raymondskill Falls, near Milford; Winona Falls, near Bushkill; and Silver Thread Falls, on Dingman's Creek, are equally well known for their majestic beauty.

The Pocono Mountains extend into Pike County, thus making it a part of Pennsylvania's best known vacationland. The county is located in the northeast section of the State, and borders parts of both New York and New Jersey. At the "Tri-States Rock," near Matamoras, visitors can stand in all three states at once.

Pike County is named for Col. Zebulon Pike, a War of 1812 hero. It was established in 1814 from parts of Wayne County. It measures 545 square miles, and is covered by forests and two large state parks. Milford is the county seat.

It was this region of the Commonwealth that nearly caused a war between the states even before the Revolution. Connecticut and Pennsylvania both laid claim to the area, and— with time out to fight the British—warred intermittently for some 30 years before Pennsylvania finally established control.

The editor of the *New York Tribune*, Horace Greeley, tried to establish an experimental community in Pike County along the lines of New England's famed Brook Farm, but Greeley's experiment failed and the community broke up in 1845.

BRIDGE BY ROEBLING—*One of the foremost engineers in America and designer of the Brooklyn Bridge, John A. Roebling, designed and built the Lackawaxen Bridge around 1850. The wooden structure is still in use today.*

Potter

One of the largest counties in the Commonwealth, Potter is located midway between the state's east and west borders and is part of Pennsylvania's northern tier along the New York state line.

Woodlots and forests make up almost half of Potter County's 1,092 square miles. And in May, the mountain laurel—the state flower—sets many of those miles ablaze with color.

The county was created in 1804 and named for General James Potter, a Revolutionary War hero. It was a pure wilderness area, a hunting ground for the Delaware Indians, and a home for timber wolves, deer, bear and mountain lions.

Its remoteness made development slow, but its timber and logging industry helped speed growth along. Today, the county is known for potatoes, paper products, leather and rubber goods. Coudersport is the county seat.

Potter is regarded as among the best hunting and fishing areas of the Commonwealth, with hundreds of thousands of acres of forests and hundreds of miles of trout streams. Its watershed has a point that drains into the St. Lawrence River, the Mississippi and the Susquehanna.

Among its points of interest is the site, near Galeton, where Ole Bull, a Norwegian violinist of worldwide fame, established a colony for his countrymen in 1852. The experiment failed after three years, however, and was moved to another state, but many descendants of the colony's founders still live in Potter County.

115 AUTUMN SCENE—Known as the "Last Frontier" of Pennsylvania, the fertile lands of Potter County provide the scene for the rich colors of Autumn. The half million acres of forest lands is an ideal area for sportsmen.

Schuylkill

Anthracite coal, allegedly discovered as a fuel source by accident, is the story of Schuylkill County. Since it was formed in 1811, the county has been a leading producer of anthracite. Its mountain ranges and coal banks, collieries and coal breakers provide a backdrop for the living legend of *King Coal,* an ever-reigning monarch in Pennsylvania.

The story is that a lumberjack named Necho Allen "discovered" in 1790 that anthracite burns. It is said that he fell asleep after building a fire among some rocks, and that when he awoke, the rocks themselves were on fire. There are other versions of how anthracite became known as a fuel source, but no matter which, if any, is fact, there is one fact—anthracite coal became a booming industry, and a lot of that industry was based in Schuylkill County.

The county is located in the central eastern part of the Commonwealth. Its name, generally assumed to be Indian, is actually Dutch, and means "hidden river" or stream. Early explorers gave the name to the Schuylkill River after failing to recognize its mouth while they were traveling up the Delaware River. Pottsville is the county seat, and is named for John Pott, pioneer operator of the famous White Horse Tavern there.

The mining industry brought all nationalities to this part of the state and their descendants and heritage remains in evidence.

COLLIERY—In 1790, lumberjack
Necho Allen built a fire among some rocks and
fell asleep. He awoke to find the rocks burning
and giving off intense heat. Today those anthracite "rocks" are still mined in open pit
mines and are Schuylkill County's chief industry.

Snyder

The Penn's Creek Massacre of 1775, believed to be the first instance of settlers slain by Indians in Pennsylvania, took place within the present borders of Snyder County. It happened a hundred years before the county was formed in 1855, and a memorial along the creek near Selinsgrove marks the site.

A central county, Snyder is an agricultural area that also produces textile goods. It measures 329 square miles, and its county seat is Middleburg, appropriately named for is central location within the county.

The county is named for Pennsylvania Governor Simon Snyder, who lived at and is buried at Selinsgrove. He served as the state's chief executive from 1808 to 1817, and was the last governor of Pennsylvania to serve three terms. His home, at 121 North Market Street, Selingsgrove, was built in 1816 and has been restored.

One of Pennsylvania's best known traditions, "Homecoming and Bean Soup," is held at McClure in the southwest corner of Snyder County. Each fall, thousands of people gather at the function, which began a hundred years ago as an annual reunion for Pennsylvania veterans of the Civil War.

Today the annual bean soup fete brings politicians from throughout the state to McClure every year. They come to test the political waters of the Commonwealth, and, of course, the bean soup.

GOVERNOR SNYDER'S HOME—Simon Snyder was the last Pennsylvania governor to serve three terms. A former Speaker of the House, and a resident of what is now Snyder County since the age of 25, Snyder's home at Selinsgrove has been preserved to honor his achievements.

VICTORIAN HOUSE PORCH — *Decorated for the celebration of the Fourth of July, picturesque*
Victorian house porches such as this one are found frequently in Snyder County.

119

Somerset

Called the *"Roof Garden of Pennsylvania,"* because its average elevation is 2,000 feet, Somerset County encompasses more than 1,000 square miles of the Commonwealth's southwest.

It was named for Somersetshire, in England, and borders in part on the state of Maryland. It was created in 1795, and Somerset, centrally located within its borders, is the county seat. At 2,250 feet elevation, it is the highest county seat in the state.

The county is Pennsylvania's leading producer of maple syrup and maple sugar. Its vast maple groves where trees are tapped for syrup in the Spring bear resemblances to parts of New England.

While Somerset County also has been an important part of the state's coal industry, it ranks first in the Commonwealth in the value of buckwheat it raises.

Mount Davis, near Myersdale, is the highest peak in Pennsylvania, rising to an elevation of 3,213 feet.

Germans and Mennonites were the principal settlers of this rugged part of the state, but the area's most prominent pioneer was Harmon Husband, a native of Maryland. He moved to Pennsylvania in 1772 with a price on his head for inciting anti-British uprisings in North Carolina.

Jeremiah Sullivan Black, U.S. Attorney General under President James Buchanan and for a brief time Secretary of State, was a native of Somerset County.

The county is a winter sports haven, and is especially known for its ski slopes at Seven Springs and Laurel Mountain.

Next page
MAPLE SYRUP—Maple syrup is made from the sap of the sugar maple tree. It takes about 128 cubic feet of wood to make 20 gallons of syrup. Scenes such as this one are commonplace in the highlands of Somerset County, Pennsylvania's leading producer of maple sugar.

Sullivan

A northeastern county just below the state's northern tier, Sullivan County is a popular recreation area that draws thousands of sports enthusiasts each year.

It is a rugged, mountainous region known for its hunting, fishing and camping as well as for several all-weather resorts.

Sullivan County was formed in 1847 and was entirely Indian land until 1768. It is named for General John Sullivan, and measures 478 square miles. Laporte is the county seat, the smallest one in the state.

Because of its vast wilderness, the county was slow in attracting settlers and in development. To help open up the territory, the state Legislature once offered land there for about six cents an acre.

But today the county has industry—farming, mining and manufacturing—as well as much of its original natural beauty. Eagles Mere Lake is known throughout the Commonwealth. And other lakes, mountain streams, state parks and dense forests make Sullivan one of the most visited counties in Pennsylvania.

Its points of interest include a natural phenomenon known as "Ticklish Rock," a large stratified rock formation that actually sways when pushed.

WATERFALL—Sullivan County was formed in 1847 and was covered with vast wilderness. Today the county has been industrialized but still retains much of its natural beauty.

Right—FISHING CREEK—The 478 square miles of Sullivan County, including 100,000 acres of state-owned forest and game lands, provides a scenic paradise for sportsmen.

Susquehanna

Susquehanna County is nearly a perfect square of 836 miles in the northeast corner of the state. It borders partly on New York and is named for the Susquehanna River, whose North Branch enters Pennsylvania in the county's own northeast corner.

Settlement did not start in Susquehanna County until after the Revolutionary War. But when the county's development began, it was farmers from New England and Quakers from southern Pennsylvania who led the way to early prosperity.

Many parts of the county bear striking similarities to New England. The county seat, Montrose, was built much like a typical New England town, and today retains much of that charm. The rural areas of the county are lined with the stone fences so often seen throughout the New England countryside.

The county is best known for its many glacial lakes and streams, its dairy farming and some anthracite coal mining. Raising turkeys and other poultry also is commercially important.

Susquehanna's most prominent citizen has been Galusha A. Grow who, at the age of 37 and at the outset of the Civil War, was elected Speaker of the U.S. House. He was a well-known freedom fighter who fathered and gained passage of the national Homestead Act, which opened the West for settlement.

One of the county's most impressive sites is the Starrucca Viaduct, a stone railroad bridge near Lanesboro. Built by the Erie Railroad Company in 1848, the bridge is 1,200 feet long, 110 feet high and 30 feet wide at the top.

WINTER—Snow covers this rural farm in Susquehanna County as the soil beneath the white cover prepares for another season of growing.

Tioga

The second largest county in the state, Tioga covers 1,150 square miles of Pennsylvania's north central mountains. A northern tier county, it is named for the Tioga River, which flows through it.

The county has more forests than fields and is abundant with big and small game. It once was almost all forest and was a hunting ground for the Seneca Indians. The logging industry claimed much of its original timber, but it still has well over a quarter of a million acres of forest land within its borders.

Pine Creek Gorge, or the *"Grand Canyon of Pennsylvania,"* also is within its borders. Fifty miles long and 1,000 feet deep, the canyon is among the most breathtaking sites of natural beauty in the Commonwealth.

Although best known for the canyon and other scenic wonders, Tioga County also is a manufacturer. At Elkland is the largest tannery of sole leather in the world. At Blossburg, bituminous coal is mined. And at Wellsboro, the county seat, is a large glassworks. The county also produces dairy products, maple syrup and natural gas.

Among Tioga's favorite sons was William B. Wilson, the first United States Secretary of Labor, serving in that post from 1913 to 1921.

GRAND CANYON—Known as "The Creator's Masterpiece in the Keystone State," the Grand Canyon was carved by the rushing waters of Pine Creek. It measures over 50 miles long, one and one half miles wide and 1,400 feet deep.

Union

Union County, located roughly in the center of the state, is known for having some of the best farmlands in Pennsylvania. It is a smaller county, measuring only 318 square miles, but is a state leader in crop production of corn, wheat and oats.

Its most fertile area is a tract called the Buffalo Valley, so named because of the herds of Pennsylvania bison that once roamed there.

Union was formed in 1813 from part of Northumberland County, one of its six neighboring counties, and was named in tribute to the then-young federation of states. Lewisburg is the county seat and the site of Northeastern Federal Penitentiary.

In addition to farming, the county's prosperity comes from the manufacture of lumber goods, especially furniture, and textile products.

There are large state parks, several dozen streams and the Susquehanna River's West Branch in Union County, all of which attract sportsmen, campers and hikers. White Deer Creek, which flows through the northern part of the county, is named for the fact that rare white deer often are seen in this area. McConnell Narrows, a popular and scenic natural monument, is located in the southwest part of the county.

Among the county's more prominent natives have been Eli Slifer, who served as Secretary of the Commonwealth under Governor Andrew Curtin during the Civil War, and Tasker H. Bliss, who was the U.S. Army Chief of Staff in World War I.

FIRST UNITED PRESBYTERIAN CHURCH—In the style most frequently associated with New England's churches, the First United Presbyterian Church of Lewisburg—built in 1857—greets the visitor with soft white Ionic columns and a regally beautiful steeple. It is the community's oldest house of Worship.

Venango

Ever since August 27, 1859, when Colonel Edwin L. Drake's oil well spewed forth 25 barrels of crude, Venango County has been the heart of Pennsylvania's lucrative oil region.

The well was built just inside Venango's northern border. Its first "rock oil" sold for about a dollar a gallon; and it started an industry that would reach worldwide importance, beyond Colonel Drake's wildest imaginings.

The natural petroleum of the Commonwealth's northwest was used by the Indians in mixing war paints, and later by settlers as a medicine called "Seneca Oil." A marker on the spot where the new industry was born and a replica of Drake's well stand today in northern Venango County.

Formed in 1800 and named the Indian word for French Creek, which flows through it, Venango has had a prosperous industrial life dominated by petroleum products and by-products. The county measures 675 square miles, and Franklin is the county seat.

There is some farming in the county, but it has been overshadowed by the role that oil has played in the overall development.

Oil boom towns came and went in Venango County as wells gushed, then dried and profiteers relocated. The principal oil town remaining is Oil City. The county gave birth to an industry whose value and significance is internationally crucial today. Drake's well was another Pennsylvania "first" that would be felt around the world for decades and centuries to come.

DRAKE'S OIL WELL—It was a well similar to this one from which oil first gushed August 27, 1859. The well was drilled by Colonel Edwin Drake, who used the 25-barrels-a-day oil output for illumination purposes.

Warren

During the first half of the 19th Century, Warren County was a logging capital. Its mills and its river rafts fed the urban centers to the south with pine to build a growing state and nation.

During the second half of the century, the county felt and became a part of the great oil boom started in nearby Venango County.

Since its inception in 1800 then, Warren County has been productive and prosperous. A northwestern county along the New York state line, Warren measures 910 square miles. It was named for the Battle of Bunker Hill hero General Joseph Warren. The county seat is Warren.

Its interests have not been limited to oil and lumber. It also has produced natural gas, metal goods and glass products.

The county remains covered by extensive timberland, including a large portion of the Allegheny National Forest. The only Indian reservation in Pennsylvania was located near Corydon, three miles south of the New York line in the county's northeastern corner. It was deeded to Cornplanter, a friendly and powerful Seneca chieftain, by George Washington and Governor Thomas Mifflin in 1790. However, with the coming of the Kinzua Dam and the huge Allegheny Reservoir, the Cornplanters were moved.

The scenic Kinzua Hills, overlooking the Allegheny Reservoir, as well as its reputation as a fishing and hunting haven, attract many sportsmen to Warren County.

129 OIL REFINERY AT NIGHT—A part of the oil boom ever since Drake's find in neighboring Venango County, Warren County still produces oil at refineries such as this one which works around-the-clock to provide Pennsylvanians with needed energy.

Washington

A typical western Pennsylvania county, Washington is a mining and manufacturing center whose importance predates the Revolutionary War.

Located in the southwest corner of the Commonwealth, it is named for the Virginia military officer who led campaigns through its present borders during the French and Indian War—General George Washington.

The county covers 857 square miles and borders partly on the state of West Virginia. It was formed in 1781, and Washington, located in the middle of the county, is its seat of government.

Because it is close to Pittsburgh and because it was blessed with a wealth of resources, Washington County always has been commercially important. Its principal products are bituminous coal, petroleum, natural gas, glassware, hay, corn and oats.

Near Washington is a monument erected by Henry Ford to honor one of the county's most prominent citizens, William Holmes McGuffey, who authored "McGuffey's Readers."

The county's interesting sites include Log Academy, which was built around 1780 near Canonsburg and which was the first school building west of the Allegheny Mountains; and Bradford House, in Washington, which was built in 1788 and which served as a command post during the Whiskey Rebellion in 1794.

TOLLHOUSE—Constructed at 15-mile intervals of the National Road built in 1806, tollhouses such as this one were used to collect monies from wagons and coaches as they passed west. In 1835 the state of Pennsylvania agreed to administer the road.

"S" BRIDGE —Named for its shape, the "S" Bridge was one of the
unique landmarks which highlighted the old National Road.

131

Wayne

Located at the northeast tip of Pennsylvania, Wayne County is a recreational area of more than 100 lakes and an historical area for literature, politics and railroading.

Named for the Revolutionary War hero General "Mad" Anthony Wayne—who died at Presque Isle in 1797—the county is covered partly by the Pocono Mountains. Its lakes and streams are well stocked and known to many fishermen. And its Lake Wallenpaupack, in the southern part of the county, is a man-made wonder 14 miles long with more than 50 miles of shore line.

The great American author Washington Irving spent much time in and around Honesdale, the county seat, and a high cliff overlooking that village has been named "Irving's Cliff."

David Wilmot, Congressman and author of the Wilmot Proviso prohibiting slavery in any new American territory, was a native of Wayne County. Wilmot, born in Bethany in 1814, is credited with establishing the foundations of the National Republican Party. Samuel Meredith, the first U.S. Treasurer, had an estate in Wayne County.

The first locomotive in America, the Stourbridge Lion—built in England—had its trial run at Honesdale in 1828. The original Lion is on display at the Smithsonian Institution in Washington, D.C., but a replica can be seen in Honesdale. Also at Honesdale is the site of the first concrete building in America. It was erected in 1857, and became the Hotel Allen.

Right—SKIING—The wooded slopes of Pennsylvania provide ideal grounds for winter sports enthusiasts. Here ski buffs enjoy their sport on Wayne County slopes.

Westmoreland

Westmoreland, or "land of the western moons," is a state leader in the production of metal and metal products, bituminous coal and aluminum.

It is the home of Henry Clay Frick, who pioneered in the iron industry, then became a partner with steel magnate Andrew Carnegie.

The county's proximity to Pittsburgh and the early navigability of the Monongahela and Allegheny Rivers served to enhance its development into one of the more productive centers in the state.

Westmoreland, named for a county in England of the same name, covers 1,025 square miles of southwest Pennsylvania. Greensburg is the center of the county, the center of the western bituminous coal fields and the county seat. New Kensington, in the northwestern part of the county along the Allegheny River, is called the "Aluminum City," and is one of the largest aluminum producing areas in the world.

Among the county's points of interest are the gravesite of General Arthur St. Clair, chairman of the Continental Congress and Governor of the Northwest Territory; the restored Fort Ligonier, which played a crucial role in Pontiac's War of 1763; Bushy Run Battlefield, north of Jeanette, where Pontiac's warriors were defeated in August of 1763; and Manor Brush Creek Church, near Manor, believed to be the oldest church west of the Allegheny Mountains.

The famous Revolutionary war flag—the Rattlesnake Flag—which bore the inscription "Don't tread on me," was carried by the Westmoreland County First Battalion.

FORT LIGONIER—Built as a staging area for General Forbes' troops before their capture of Fort Dusquesne on November 25, 1758, Fort Ligonier was the only stronghold that did not fall during the Pontiac Revolt of 1763.

Wyoming

A northeastern county that still reflects its New England and American Indian heritage in the names of many of its municipalities, Wyoming County was formed in 1842 and named for Pennsylvania's historic Wyoming Valley.

The North Branch of the Susquehanna River, which flows through the county, provides Wyoming with rich soil and helps make the area a prosperous one for dairy farming, apples and poultry.

Flagstone is one of its most famous products, and is exported to all parts of the United States. But lumber, leather products, rubber goods and gravel also are produced there.

The county is situated on a plateau and is covered by many lakes, including Lake Winola and Lake Carey. It measures 396 square miles, and Tunkhannock is the county seat.

Near the northern border at Nicholson stands a two-track railroad viaduct. The concrete structure, which was built in 1915, crosses Tunkhannock Creek. It is 2,375 feet long and 243 feet high.

At Laceyville, in the extreme northwest corner of the county, is a frame house built in 1790 completely without nails.

One of major league baseball's greatest pitchers, Christy Mathewson, was born at Factoryville, near the county's eastern border.

HERDING DOWN THE ROAD—Susquehanna County is a leader in the state in value of cattle and milk produced. Dairy herds are led each day to the pasturelands for grazing and watering in the rich and fertile lands of the region.

York

Picturesque, historical York County lies in the south central section of the state, west of the Susquehanna River.

It covers 914 square miles of fine farm land, but also is known as a great industrial area of Pennsylvania.

Formed in 1749 and named for the city of York in England, the county is famous for all types of agricultural crops as well as for the manufacture of heavy machinery, textiles, furniture, cigars and paper products.

York, the county seat, served as the Capital of the United States from September of 1777 to June of 1778 during the British occupation of Philadelphia. The Congress met at that time in the York County Courthouse in the center of the city.

York had its own liberty bell which summoned the Congress to session and later proclaimed national independence. The bell is retained in a York church as an historical artifact.

The first Civil War battle north of the Mason-Dixon line took place at Hanover before the Battle of Gettysburg.

Among the county's many points of interest is a Society of Friends Meeting House in York that has been in continuous use since 1765; and the site of the Codorus Furnace, the oldest remaining landmark to the county's once-lucrative iron industry. Erected in 1765, the furnace was used to re-equip General George Washington's army at Valley Forge.

PLOUGH TAVERN —Gates House in York was named for General Horatio Gates, head of the Revolutionary Board of War. The Plough Tavern, built in 1741, was the site of the Marquis de Lafayette's toast to General George Washington which ended the Conway Cabal, an attempt to oust Washington as Commander-in-chief.

STATE FLOWER —By Act of the Assembly No. 107, approved May 5, 1933, Pennsylvania adopted the Mountain Laurel (Kalmia latifolia) as the state flower.

STATE BIRD—By Act No. 234 of the General Assembly, approved June 22, 1931, Pennsylvania adopted the "king of the game birds," the Ruffed Grouse, (Bonasa umbellus) as the state bird.

STATE TREE AND STATE ANIMAL—By Act No. 233, approved June 22, 1931, the General Assembly selected the Hemlock (Tsuga canadensis Linnaeus) as the state tree. On October 2, 1959, the General Assembly passed Act No. 416 selecting the White Tail Deer as the state animal.

PENNSYLVANIA: A COMMEMORATIVE PORTRAIT ----- INDEX

PENNSYLVANIA: A COMMEMORATIVE PORTRAIT ----- ILLUSTRATIONS